The Catholics
and their Houses

Catholic Houses in Great Britain

1 Warblington Castle, Hampshire
2 Hendred House, Berkshire
3 Stonor Park, Oxfordshire
4 Oxburgh hall, Norfolk
5 Broughton Hall, Yorkshire
6 Norbury Manor, Derbyshire
7 Baddersley Clinton, Warwickshire

8 Hoghton Tower, Lancashire
9 Mapledurham, Berkshire
10 Coughton Court, Warwickshire
11 Wardour, Wiltshire
12 Boscobel, Shropshire
13 Warley Hall, Greater Manchester
14 Traquair House, Peebleshire

15 Ince Blundell Hall, Merseyside
16 Ingatestone Hall, Essex
17 Stonyhurst, Lancashire
18 Grace Dieu Manor, Leicestershire
19 Mount Stuart, Isle of Bute
20 Tichborne House, Hampshire

The CATHOLICS AND THEIR HOUSES

Leanda de Lisle and Peter Stanford

Photographs by Richard Surman

with a Foreword by
the Duke of Norfolk

HarperCollins*Publishers*

To Peter and Siobhan
our respective – and ever supportive – spouses

HarperCollins*Publishers*
77-85 Fulham Palace Road, London W6 8JB

First published in Great Britain
in 1995 by HarperCollins*Publishers*

1   3   5   7   9   10   8   6   4   2

Copyright in the text © 1995 by Leanda de Lisle and Peter Stanford
Copyright © in the photographs Richard Surman

Leanda de Lisle and Peter Stanford assert the moral right
to be identified as the authors of this work

A catalogue record for this book is
available from the British Library

0 00 627924 4

Produced by HarperCollins Hong Kong

CONTENTS

The Eighteenth Century: out of the shadows

The Nineteenth Century:
emancipation and the reconversion of England?

Foreword

BY HIS GRACE THE DUKE OF NORFOLK

WE ARE fortunate to live in an age of religious tolerance. Today no one can legitimately be denied a job or the right to hold property on account of their faith. Sadly it has not always been so. From the time of Henry VIII's break from Rome in 1534 through to the Catholic Emancipation Act of 1829, with a brief but bloody interval during the reign of Mary Tudor, many who tried to balance loyalty to the Crown with fidelity to the Pope in matters of conscience suffered as a consequence.

Among them were some of my own ancestors, like Philip Howard, the Earl of Arundel, who died in the Tower of London in 1595 for keeping his Catholic faith. His wife, the Countess, was stripped of much of her income but allowed her London residence, Howard House in the Strand, to be used as a refuge for Catholic priests like Father Robert Southwell about whom we read in these pages. Such recusant priests, trained on the Continent, travelled round the country incognito, saying Mass, hiding away from the authorities. If they were caught, they faced trial and execution.

A flavour of those terrible times can be sampled at the house in which I grew up, Carlton Towers, near Goole in Yorkshire. Though much of the house was rebuilt in Victorian times, one of its wings dates back to the seventeenth century. Hollowed out of the main chimney stack is a hiding place, reached via a trapdoor on the top floor in a room which was once part of the Long Gallery. Here it is believed Catholic priests sheltered from the eagle eye of the authorities.

There are many other, sometimes little noticed, houses around the country that boast such unusual architectural features and this book collects their remarkable stories in one volume for the first time. The authors have done an admirable job of recreating the atmosphere of the times through the histories of various Catholic families.

Though both Catholics, Leanda de Lisle and Peter Stanford tell this tale without any hint of bitterness or recrimination. Rather they treat their subject as a fascinating though too often forgotten period of history. They bring it to life in a novel and entertaining way by focusing on the houses where Catholicism was never quite extinguished and on the colourful and courageous individuals who passed through their portals.

Tolerance does not require us to be blind to past excesses. Indeed it demands the opposite. We have to recognize where we went wrong to ensure that we never do so again. This book allows its readers to dip into a tragic period of history without ever preaching at them. I can heartily recommend it.

INTRODUCTION

Ours is not a bad story. No Church has been so persecuted for so long. And everyone knows about John Fisher and Thomas More. They're household names. There's a great respect for that tradition.
Cardinal Basil Hume

In the marmoreal interior of Westminster Cathedral, the neo-Byzantine mother church of English Catholicism, there is a list of the 'Chief Pastors of the Catholic Church in England showing their communion with the Apostolic See of Rome'. It starts with Augustine of Canterbury in 601 but breaks off abruptly with Thomas Cranmer, deprived of the seals of office by the Pope in 1533. Cranmer was prepared to allow Henry VIII to divorce his first wife Catherine of Aragon and marry Anne Boleyn. The Pope was not. Henry's decision to name Cranmer as Archbishop of Canterbury formally opened the breach between the English Crown and the papacy which remains to this day.

Caught up in this battle, torn between their allegiance to their king and their fidelity to the Pope, were the recusant Catholics. A small group of interconnected, well-to-do families, they tried to balance civil and religious obligations. When they failed, they put the spiritual above the secular and for three centuries after the Reformation they kept the flame of the one true faith flickering in the priest-holes of their country houses. This book tells their story through those houses.

By their recusancy, they risked life and limb to maintain their allegiance to the Pope at a time when the English Crown had asserted its supremacy in matters of religion. To shelter a Catholic priest was treason, punishable by death. At the very least failure to conform with the 'new' religion incurred penal taxation, travel restrictions and a bar on a career in government or the military.

The sons of recusant families had to escape to the Continent to get a Catholic education with the Jesuits at Saint Omer in northern France while their daughters went to convents in what is today Belgium. The Catholic families intermarried, partly because recusant society was in a constant state of siege and outsiders were viewed with suspicion, and partly because no self-respecting Protestant grandee would welcome a match with papist outcasts. Those sons who did not marry studied for the priesthood at seminaries at Douai in France, Rome, Lisbon or Valladolid in Spain and then returned by cover of night to celebrate the Eucharist in their family homes and those of trusted neighbours.

To be caught was to face martyrdom on the gallows at Tyburn and elsewhere. The successful faced a life forever on the run, continually flitting from one secret Mass centre to another, avoiding the attention of the pursuivants or priest-hunters, eschewing any religious title or trappings, to bring spiritual sustenance to a fearful but determined flock.

The struggle went on, with varying degrees of intensity, until the Catholic Emancipation Act of 1829. The earliest martyrs to the cause of an English Roman Catholic Church died in 1535 under Henry VIII. Amongst them were Thomas More and Bishop John Fisher, executed in the Tower of

London for their refusal to sign the Act of Supremacy which proclaimed Henry head of the Church. Their stories are linked with Hendred House as we will see later.

If the Oath of Supremacy began the process of distancing the Catholic families from the Crown, the Dissolution of the Monasteries accelerated it. Henry's brutal and avaricious attack on the properties of the Church started in 1535 and galvanized his opponents into acts of defiance – like the Pilgrimage of Grace of 1536 – and widespread dissent.

The Catholic families were in the forefront of efforts to persuade – or force – the King to change course. Reginald Pole, later a cardinal and in 1549 almost Pope, became a leader of the opposition in exile, firing verbal volleys at Henry from the safety of Rome while his saintly mother, Margaret Pole of Warblington Castle, once a royal favourite, was hacked to death in 1541 by an inexperienced axeman.

Henry was succeeded by his son Edward VI in 1547, and the Protestant hue of the English Reformation deepened. On his death the Crown passed – after a brief attempt to install the Protestant Lady Jane Grey on the throne – to Mary Tudor. Her succession marked the first of the great swings in fortune for the Catholic families. Catherine of Aragon's daughter was determined to restore England to the Pope. With Pole at her right hand, she presided – some say reluctantly – over the burning of 300 Protestants in a brutal counter-offensive which claimed in three years more lives than the Spanish Inquisition during an entire century. In mourning the English Catholic martyrs, the victims of 'Bloody Mary' must never be forgotten. Both suffered the intolerance of the Tudors.

When Elizabeth first came to the throne in 1558 her intentions were unclear. A pragmatist more interested in matters of state than of the soul, she had to contend with the large number of Marian favourites who remained in positions of influence at her court. The Queen therefore promised a broad religious settlement but such pledges were not enough for those who wanted to see Henry's work unpicked. The Catholic families rallied to this opposition and came increasingly to pin their hopes on the romantic but tragic figure of Mary Queen of Scots who arrived in England in 1568.

Yet conspiracy after conspiracy in pursuit of such a goal failed and with each failure the English queen's patience with the recusant Catholics diminished. It was not so much their religion that she objected to as their treachery and their determination to unseat her. The Great Northern Rising of 1569 attracted support from recusants like the Tempests of Broughton Hall. The Throckmorton Plot of 1585 compromised the family whose name it annexed and threatened their home at Coughton Court, a centre of secret Jesuit activity.

Outside forces too pushed Elizabeth onto the defensive. The Pope excommunicated her in 1570 in what subsequent generations have regarded as a fatal – literally for many a Jesuit – miscalculation. The Spanish Armada of 1588 attempted an invasion to overthrow her and prompted a fivefold increase in executions of priests and those who helped them.

The previous year Elizabeth had reluctantly agreed to the death of Mary Queen of Scots, the Catholic heir apparent, mementos of whose long years in captivity are treasured at Oxburgh Hall. Though Mary's death was a bitter blow to Catholic hopes, many in the recusant camp had long since realized that they had to explore other ways to undermine Elizabeth's religious policies.

In 1568 Cardinal William Allen, near neighbour and friend of the Hoghtons of Hoghton Tower, had set up the seminary at Douai to train young men to replace the dwindling band of Marian priests in ministering to the Catholic community.

Five years later as the first products emerged from its classrooms the Catholic Church was fast disappearing underground. The new generation of young Jesuit priests, men like Robert Southwell and John Gerard, went round in mufti, serving private chapels in the Catholic houses like Stonor Park and Baddesley Clinton. By night they sheltered in priest-holes fashioned by the master craftsman Nicholas 'Little John' Owen. Many − like Edmund Campion, one of Elizabeth's most articulate and cunning opponents − were caught and died long-drawn-out and painful deaths.

By the end of Elizabeth's reign some 800 seminary priests had been smuggled into England of whom about 300 were still at large. She had executed 123 priests and more than 60 lay Catholics. Though they did not die in vain, the outcome of Elizabeth's terror should not be underestimated. When she succeeded England had been a Catholic country with a committed minority of Protestants. At her death in 1603, Catholics were in the minority and the moderate Protestantism of the national Church was the norm.

Hopes that James I might be more amenable to Catholics proved ill-founded. The Gunpowder Plot of 1605, a thwarted papist conspiracy aimed at blowing up the Houses of Parliament, served to unleash a new wave of persecution against Catholics, a fifth column to be rooted out and punished.

With the dawn of the seventeenth century, the net tightened around the recusants. Some like the Blounts of Mapledurham had managed hitherto to be outwardly faithful to the Crown while guarding their private conscience. But increasingly such a double life was impossible. The Catholics retired to their estates, kept their heads down and struggled to pay the fines that were heaped upon them. While their Anglican neighbours updated their houses in line with the latest architectural fashions, Catholic homes like Baddesley Clinton remained caught in a time-warp, sombre, threadbare and unmodernized.

There was a fluctuation under Charles I when the king took up arms against his Parliament in 1642. Charles had not been notably kind to Catholics. In 1641, for instance, the Jesuit Ambrose Barlow, whose skull is thought to reside at Wardley Hall, was executed and his head paraded through Manchester. Yet suddenly Charles needed all the support he could muster, while the recusant families, whatever his past mistreatment of them, realized that the monarch, with his Catholic wife, was infinitely preferable to the Puritan Roundheads. These religious extremists demonized Catholics and took apparent pleasure in wiping out the Irish Catholic camp followers of the Royalist army.

However, as Charles stumbled in battle, the great Catholic houses like Wardour were besieged and overrun by Parliamentary forces. Again it was Catholics who gave succour to Charles's son as he attempted in 1651 to reclaim his throne. When he took refuge at Boscobel after the Battle of Worcester, it was a Catholic family that protected him. Once crowned in 1660 though, Charles was half-hearted in repaying his old allies. Despite his own Catholic convictions, he gave credence in 1678 to a 'popish plot' against him, 'revealed' by the fraudster Titus Oates. The king threw various recusant notables like Lord Petre into the Tower of London.

The advent of James II in 1685 marked another upturn in Catholic fortunes. Once again the old families could look to employment at court or in the military. Some undertook substantial building works at their homes. It proved a short-lived new dawn. In 1688 the 'Glorious Revolution' chased James off his throne, while mobs destroyed new and restored Catholic chapels at Hendred and Coughton. At the Battle of the Boyne two years later James's hopes of a return were finally extinguished.

William and Mary, installed as monarchs by Parliament, and avowed Protestants, ushered in a new round of anti-Catholic legislation. Attempts at uprisings by James's son – in 1715 – and his grandson, Bonnie Prince Charlie – in 1745 – left their mark on homes like Traquair, in Scotland, but failed to revive the notion of a Catholic monarchy. That died for ever in the eighteenth century.

As the years progressed, however, there was a gradual relaxation of anti-Catholic measures. The Relief Acts of 1778 and 1791 allowed Catholics property rights and the freedom to run their own schools. Stonyhurst, a recusant fortress in Lancashire, was taken over by the Jesuits as their base for educating the children of the old families. And at nearby Ince Blundell, one of the centres of the Jesuit mission in Lancashire, the recusant owners were confident enough to build themselves an impressive new home.

The chapel significantly was kept hidden in a gable end. The Gordon Riots of 1778 illustrated that a virulent strain of anti-Catholicism still lived in the popular mind. The recusants as a consequence did well to avoid flaunting their religious practice lest it be judged proselytizing. Relaxation in the penal laws did not bring acceptability. Those who paid homage to the Pope were known as Roman Catholics. The Puritan poet John Milton scoffed at the title, calling it one of the Pope's bulls. For society at large the name carried with it an air of foreignness, of a narrow sect like today's Seventh-Day Adventists.

Full civil liberties came in 1829 – the by-product of events in British-ruled but overwhelmingly Catholic Ireland – and many of the recusant families dusted down their uniforms and returned to serve the Crown at court or in county government. The 1829 act allowed Catholics once more to take their seats in the House of Lords, but only six peers with the right remained – Clifford, Dormer, Norfolk, Petre, Stafford and Stourton.

Catholic ranks were given an infusion of new blood with a steady stream of notable converts in the Victorian age. Yet when wealthy young men from influential Establishment families like Ambrose de Lisle of Grace Dieu Manor and the Marquis of Bute of Mount Stuart came over to Rome, there was disquiet in the ruling classes and outrage in the popular press. John Henry Newman's abandonment of the Oxford Movement and reception into the Catholic Church in 1845 was as much debated as crossing the floor of the House of Commons would be today.

The Pope restored the Catholic hierarchy in 1850 and his choice of Nicholas Wiseman as the first Archbishop of Westminster only served to exacerbate Anglican fury. Wiseman's regal manner and his insensitive comments angered everyone – including the recusant families. The crowds came out in force with cries of 'No Popery'. There were questions in Parliament, bitter words of recrimination from the Prime Minister, Lord Russell, and leaders in the *Times* condemning 'the grossest act of folly and impertinence which the court of Rome has ventured to commit since the crown and people of England threw off its yoke'.

Faced with such blatant anti-Catholic feelings, the recusant families continued by and large to keep a low profile. In 1871 a celebrated court case was brought by a butcher from Wagga Wagga who claimed to be the heir to the recusant stronghold of Tichborne House. The resulting furore revealed once again how fragile was the tolerance that the Church of Rome had achieved.

It was not until the twentieth century that the English Catholic Church began to hold its head up in public once more. By that time successive waves of Irish immigration throughout the nineteenth century changed the topography of Catholic England. The vast majority of believers suddenly had more in common with the old Irishers who built the railways in Flora Thompson's *Lark Rise to Candleford* than the aristocratic Flytes of Evelyn Waugh's 1944 'Catholic' novel, *Brideshead Revisited*. With the growth of the

Catholic education system in the post-1945 era bringing prosperity and embourgeoisement, English Catholicism has moved into the mainstream of national life, a middle-class Church whose current leader, Cardinal Basil Hume, is at home in Establishment circles.

Though the persecutions have ended, the old recusant families and their homes still remain, a testament to an unhappy chapter in national life and to an enduring faith every bit as strong as that which has recently re-emerged after years of Communist persecution behind the Iron Curtain. Recusant scions may now have abandoned the tradition of unions with other Catholic families and 'married out' into the emerging Catholic middle class. The old names have been mixed in with wealthy Catholic entrepreneurs like the Gilbeys or glamorous twentieth-century converts like Waugh himself or the Longford clan.

Yet there are still those who can today trace their ancestors back to Catholicism's darkest hour. Once a year they gather in London to commemorate the past. A direct line back to the times of Henry VIII is the *sine qua non* of membership of the exclusive 15 Club, where, under the Presidency of the Duke of Norfolk, Britain's leading Catholic layman, a toast is drunk to the health of the Pope.

In telling this story of faith through the medium of bricks and mortar, we have attempted – appropriately – to build one block at a time, starting with the houses whose most dramatic events occurred at the beginning of the age of persecution and working our way via various locations through to the Victorian age. Some of the properties have interesting tales to impart in several of the different periods under review and there is, inevitably, a degree of overlap, of one step forward and two steps back.

The choice of houses is, at the end of the day, an idiosyncratic and very personal one. Some famous names like the ruined Lulworth Castle in

Dorset, home to the Welds, and Plowden in Shropshire, will have to wait until, God willing, volume two. Our one regret is the omission in this volume of any house in Wales, though Cardiff Castle does figure in the story of Mount Stuart.

A final thought: throughout much of what follows some readers may be haunted by the faces of Jeremy Irons and Anthony Andrews from the celebrated early 1980s television dramatization of Evelyn Waugh's *Brideshead Revisited*. Waugh's novel is often mistakenly assumed to be a picture of a recusant family and their home.

While the fictional Brideshead itself contains elements of Wardour Castle – which Waugh visited in 1944 – its Arts-and-Crafts chapel is quite unlike Wardour's and rather more akin to that at Madresfield, home to Waugh's Anglican friends the Lygons.

And the Flytes, at the centre of the novel, may don their mantillas for Mass in the family chapel of their ancestral pile, but they are parvenus, recent converts to Rome through Lady Marchmain, herself a rather too haughty and grand character to be a credible representative of the venerable but often hard-pressed Catholic clans.

This book is not then a vision of Brideshead, but a glimpse of something older, less ostentatious and more courageous.

THREE CENTURIES OF TURMOIL AND TORMENT IN THE NAME OF RELIGION

1509 – Henry VIII succeeds his father as King of England

1529 – Wolsey fails to get papal approval for royal divorce

1533 – Henry marries Anne Boleyn

1534 – Henry breaks with Rome and orders Oath of Supremacy

1535 – Dissolution of the Monasteries

1535 – Thomas More and John Fisher executed

1536 – Pilgrimage of Grace protests at Henry's religious policies

1547 – Henry dies and is succeeded by Edward VI

1549 – Use of Book of Common Prayer made compulsory

1553 – Edward dies

1553 – Attempt by Protestants to place Lady Jane Grey on throne fails

1553 – Mary Tudor succeeds her half-brother

1555 – Execution of Protestant dissenters begins

1558 – Mary dies and is succeeded by Elizabeth

1559 – Act of Uniformity introduces fines for Catholics

1563 – Thirty-Nine Articles issued as summary of Anglicanism

1568 – Mary Queen of Scots arrives in England

1568 – Seminary opens at Douai in France for English 'mission'

1569 – Rising of nobles in the North in support of Mary crushed

1570 – Pope excommunicates Elizabeth

1573 – First Douai priests arrive

1581 – Secret printing of Father Campion's 'Ten Reasons'

1581 – Campion caught and executed

1585 – Throckmorton Plot prompts new anti-Catholic laws

1586 – Secret Harleyford Conference on renewed missionary campaign

1586 – Babington Plot foiled

1587 – Mary Queen of Scots executed

1588 – Spanish Armada defeated

1593 – Five Mile Act restricts movement of Catholics

1593 – Jesuits establish school at Saint Omer for English Catholics

1603 – Elizabeth dies and is succeeded by James I

1605 – Guy Fawkes' Gunpowder Plot foiled

1642 – Civil War breaks out

1649 – Charles I beheaded and Commonwealth declared

1660 – Monarchy restored under Charles II

1678 – Titus Oates 'reveals' Popish Plot

1685 – Charles dies and is succeeded by Catholic James II

1688 – 'Glorious Revolution' brings Protestant William and Mary to throne

1690 – James defeated at the Battle of the Boyne and exiled

1692 – Double land tax imposed on Catholics

1715 – Failed Jacobite rebellion under James's son, James The Old Pretender

1745 – Bonnie Prince Charlie's Stuart rising fails

1778 – First Catholic Relief Act prompts Gordon Riots

1785 – Future George IV secretly marries Catholic Mrs Fitzherbert

1791 – Second Catholic Relief Act

1829 – Catholic Emancipation Act

1845 – John Henry Newman converts to Catholicism

1850 – Pope Pius IX restores the English and Welsh hierarchy

1935 – Fisher and More declared saints by the Pope

1966 – Archbishop of Canterbury visits the Pope in Rome

1970 – Canonization of 40 post-Reformation martyrs

1982 – Pope John Paul II visits Canterbury Cathedral

1987 – Beatification of 85 English and Welsh post-Reformation martyrs

THE SIXTEENTH CENTURY

REFORMATION, REBELLION AND RECUSANCY

WARBLINGTON CASTLE

HAMPSHIRE

Behold how first the modest Rose doth pry,
Out of her summer coat in virgin's hour,
One half in sight, half-hidden from the eye,
The lesser seen, the fairer to view
Robert Southwell SJ

A RUINED turret, a tiny timbered spire and a gateway, framed by the wide inlet of Chichester Harbour, are all that remain of Warblington Castle, an unreformed bastion of Catholic England until its destruction in 1644.

A survey conducted in the early part of the seventeenth century describes the castle as 'two hundred feet square, with a fair green court within and buildings round the said court; with a fair gallery and divers chambers and two towers covered with lead; a very great and spacious hall, parlour and a great chamber with a chapel and all other offices'.

Warblington's coastal setting, facing out onto Hayling Island, and its rose-filled gardens are thought to have proved an inspiration to the Jesuit poet Robert Southwell, who visited the castle as a young man. One of his biographers suggests that Southwell was haunted by 'memories of a casement window opening in the early morning on tree-tops and meadows and a walled garden; of brocaded dresses in the afternoon like moving rose-bushes; of a golden sunset fading over mellow walls and feathery orchards'.

The ruined turret is one of four that once stood at right angles to the castle itself. It remains a shrine to Margaret Pole whose home Warblington was. A descendant of the royal house of Plantagenet, the daughter of George, Duke of Clarence, and the niece of Edward IV and Richard III, she was destined like so many in her family to die at the hands of a king. Her uncle, Edward IV, had her father killed by being drowned, as legend has it, in a butt of his favourite Malmsey wine. Anxious to eliminate all other rivals for the throne, Henry VII had her brother, Edward, Earl of Warwick, imprisoned in the Tower of London and beheaded in 1499.

Catherine of Aragon believed that the Earl's death had been caused, indirectly, by her father, King Ferdinand. He had refused to give her in marriage to Henry's son while a male Plantagenet pretender was still alive. In later life Catherine grew to believe that all her troubles had arisen because her marriage to the future Henry VIII was 'made in blood' and the Queen therefore lavished attention on Warwick's widowed sister, Margaret Pole, and her four sons and daughter. Margaret was made godmother – and later governess – to Catherine's daughter, the future Queen Mary.

Henry VIII too held Margaret in high regard, once describing her as the most saintly woman in England. He awarded her a pension, made her Countess of Salisbury and restored to her in 1514 various Plantagenet estates, including Warblington.

Margaret Pole had scarcely completed remodelling Warblington when Henry decided to divorce Catherine. Margaret, a staunch Catholic, opposed the king and refused to acknowledge Anne Boleyn as queen in 1533. To avoid being pressurized to compromise her principles, she retired from court to her moated castle on the south coast.

Her son Reginald, once a royal favourite, fled into exile, but he kept in close touch with his family at Warblington – using a local man, Hugh Holland, who had previous convictions for piracy, as his messenger. Then in 1536 he unleashed – from the safety of Rome where he had been created a cardinal by the Pope – a document, *Unititate Ecclesiae*, which lambasted everything Henry had done to the Church.

In his rage the King turned on Margaret Pole and the rest of her family, warning the French ambassador that he intended to kill the lot of them. Margaret's son Geoffrey, her son-in-law Henry, Lord Montague, his cousin Henry Courtney, the Marquis of Exeter and their friend Sir Edward Neville were all arrested.

Geoffrey was forced to turn king's evidence and this was enough to condemn them all to death in 1539. Even their children did not escape the royal wrath. Montague's son was put in the Tower of London, never to be seen again, while Lord Exeter's child spent his whole childhood and adolescence there before finally being released by Mary when she became queen in 1553. The pathetic inscriptions carved by these children on the walls of their dungeons can still be seen.

Geoffrey survived, a pariah with the blood of his family on his hands. He spent the rest of his life wandering around Europe demented with remorse.

Margaret's grief was not remorse enough for the king and ten days after the rest of her family had been seized, the Bishop of Ely arrived at Warblington to arrest a woman who had been a second mother to the king's daughter.

Margaret refused to admit to any Catholic plot against the king or indeed any other wrongdoing. She was therefore condemned without trial by Bill of Attainder on June 28, 1539. She remained in the Tower for two years, tormented by the cold and damp, until early on the morning of May 27, 1541, she was led out to die.

The executioner, young, inexperienced and some say drunk, took half a dozen blows to complete his task. Margaret Pole's death remains one of the blackest spots on Henry VIII's character.

She had prepared a beautiful chantry as her last resting place at Christchurch Priory but with considerable spite Henry insisted that she be buried in Saint Peter's in the Tower. Her property was seized and Warblington passed through various hands until in 1551 it was granted to Sir Richard Cotton.

Reginald Pole never forgave Henry his crime. When in 1554 he returned to England to assist Queen Mary in the restoration of Catholicism, succeeding Thomas Cranmer as Archbishop of Canterbury two years later, the cardinal reputedly took his revenge. Sir Francis Englefield claimed to have been present at Windsor when the Queen and Pole had Henry's embalmed body disinterred and burned.

In 1555, with Pole's enthusiastic support, Mary began burning Protestant dissenters as heretics. By the time of her death three years later, she had claimed some 300 victims, a third of them clergy and a fifth women. In June 1557, the Pope reprimanded Pole on charges of heresy and demanded that he return to Rome. Mary refused to let him go but in November of the following year, on hearing news that his queen had died while at Mass in Saint James's Palace, the cardinal himself expired, a victim, it was said, of grief, overwork and the fever.

Under the Cottons, like the Poles unreformed Catholics, Warblington's traditions were maintained. Sir Richard died in 1556 and passed the property to his son, George. A man of considerable wealth, he was one of the few recusants to pay the full fine of £20 a month imposed on Catholics by

Mary's successor, her half-sister Elizabeth. At the same time he continued in defiance of the law to maintain his own Catholic chaplain at Warblington and to attend Masses. As Elizabeth's attitude to such dissent hardened in the later years of her reign, Cotton was arrested and held in Fleet Jail. He died a prisoner in 1610.

Warblington under the Cottons was a vital – though secret – staging post on the route to and from the Continent when after 1574 Jesuit priests began crossing the Channel to keep the old faith alive in England. The castle's position on Chichester Harbour made it a perfect alternative to the busy ports, a safe haven for boats from France.

In 1576 the young Robert Southwell, whose mother was a cousin of George Cotton, sailed from Warblington to France to train as a Jesuit priest at the newly-established seminary at Douai. Ten years later Southwell returned, after a spell in charge of studies at the English College in Rome, to spearhead the Jesuit mission. For almost a decade he travelled all over the country, often using the alias Cotton and sheltering in a succession of hides – or priest-holes – in the homes of Catholic families still loyal to the Pope. In 1595, he was captured and executed.

Like many other Catholics, the Cottons forgot past differences with the Crown and sided with Charles I in the Civil War against Cromwell. In January 1644, Warblington was captured by the Puritan Roundheads from its Royalist defenders and destroyed. Its stones are said to have been used to build a street in nearby Portsmouth.

The turret and gatehouse, close to the fourteenth-century church that Margaret Pole would have used, stand as a monument to a faith that refused to be broken in a brutal age of intolerance. They were maintained down the centuries as a navigational landmark on Chichester Harbour. Today the castle is in the hands of the Bishop family who live in a house near the ruin.

Hendred House

BERKSHIRE

Saint Thomas More, by his line of defence, his prose style and his personal legend, encouraged the families of the ancient faith in their perseverance. The possession of certain relics, the inheritance of a strain of blood and the present strength of his memory aided his co-religionists who were so strongly bound together by common suffering and exclusion. In the periods when their contact with the active national life was most fettered, Saint Thomas More remained their solitary hero to receive recognition from the average Englishman. *Archbishop David Mathew*

As you enter the front hall at Hendred House in the Vale of the White Horse, your eyes are drawn upwards towards the massive fifteenth-century beams that still hold together the early medieval wattle-and-daub walls. Hanging on the stairwell is a life-sized portrait of Thomas More with his children. As this great Englishman gazes out, he must feel at home for here, as in so many of the Catholic houses, time has stood still since the Reformation.

The Eyston family, whose seat this has been since the fifteenth century, remained unflinchingly Catholic through good times and bad, though their fidelity to Rome cost them dear. Penalized by anti-Catholic taxes and denied well-paid employment at court or in the military on account of their beliefs, they were never rich enough to update Hendred House to match the refinements of neighbouring Thames Valley squires. The result is that Hendred House has the feel of a time capsule.

Among its treasures are reminders of two of the earliest and best-known martyrs to the Catholic cause, Thomas More and John Fisher, canonised by the Pope in 1935. Fisher, Bishop of Rochester in Kent, was an intensely spiritual man who kept away from the royal court, preferring, as the historian Robert Lacey describes, to 'eat alone in his great draughty palace...with only a skull for company at his table, while a priest read Gregorian homilies to him'.

Almost alone of the bench of bishops, Fisher refused to sanction Henry VIII's break with Rome by taking the Oath of Supremacy. Furthermore he acted as confessor to Catherine of Aragon, the king's discarded first wife. While Rome applauded his courage and made him a cardinal, Henry's response was to order his execution, declaring that he would send the Pope Fisher's head so that he could personally place a cardinal's red hat on it.

In his mid seventies when he died in June 1535, Fisher used an ebony walking stick to stagger to the block at Tower Hill in London. This is now kept at Hendred House. It was claimed after Fisher's death by his successor, John Hildesley, a Dominican friar, whose family remained staunchly Catholic. They kept the stick as a reminder of Fisher and it is believed to have passed to the Eystons when Mary Hildesley married into the family at the end of the seventeenth century.

More was a very different man from Fisher. Celebrated to this day, notably in the play and film *A Man for All Seasons*, he was known throughout Europe as a brilliant lawyer and academic. An affectionate family man, free with his money and possessed of a refined sense of humour, he joined the cardinal in refusing to swear the Oath and was executed at Tower Hill two weeks after him.

More's image appears in all the major rooms at Hendred, here in a portrait, there in an engraving. There is also what Thomas Eyston, the current owner, calls 'a first class relic' – a conveyance document from More's house in London, Crosby Hall, complete with his signature and personal seal. With this is kept More's drinking cup, a simple tankard of dark wood, with silver rings bearing a hallmark from Henry VII's reign. The cup was left to the Eyston family by Maria Theresa Metcalfe, his descendant, who married Charles Eyston in 1814.

She was responsible for renovations to Hendred House's thirteenth-century chapel – one of only three in the country to have remained exclusively Catholic since the Reformation. Like much of the house, its story is revealing of the fortunes of Catholics in England in the post-Reformation period.

During the reign of Edward VI, the Chantry of Saint Amand – to give the chapel its full name – was stripped of its glebe and tythe lands and disguised as a woodshed. Thomas Eyston believes that this proved a useful disguise while worship carried on unobserved. He points out a place in the gallery where a secret door led to a priests' hiding place.

With the advent of the Catholic James II in 1685 and hope of an age of positive discrimination in favour of their fellow believers, the Eystons began restoration works. 'My father, George Eyston, Esquire, beagan the Repaire of this Chappell on Wednesday in Easter weeke in ye yeare 1687', Charles Eyston later wrote. 'One Andrew Bartlet painted and guilded it... From the time of its being opened till the Prince of Orange came in and invaded the Nation, the Chappell was open to all Commers and goers.'

In 1688 the 'Glorious Revolution' replaced James II with William III, Prince of Orange, and his wife Mary and ushered in one of the fiercest periods of Catholic persecution in English history. The invading army stopped at Hendred House, sacked the chapel, celebrated a travesty of the Mass and stole the priest's vestments. These were taken to Oxford where they were put on a dummy which was then publicly burnt.

In recent years much work has been undertaken and the house has been completely restored. Hendred House, however, remains the family home and is not open to the public. Mass is still said in the chapel at least once a week – usually Friday. The current incumbent is a former Anglican vicar who converted to Catholicism and was ordained a priest. The irony would not have been lost on Thomas More.

STONOR PARK

OXFORDSHIRE

Rain, rain on Tyburn tree
Red rain a-falling
Dew, dew on Tyburn tree
And the swart bird a-calling
Francis Thompson's 'Ode to the English Martyrs'

THERE can be few places where the history of the Catholic persecution is so tangible as at Stonor Park in Oxfordshire. This elegant house with its skin of faded Tudor brick lies long and low, rooted in the Chiltern Hills, overlooking a valley that seems the very quintessence of the English landscape. Deer have grazed there since the time of the Plantagenets. Yet in the last decades of the sixteenth century Stonor struggled behind its tranquil exterior to cling to the faith of ages in the face of Henry VIII's break with Rome.

No threat could coerce Stonor to follow the king in matters of religion though it remained true to him on all other questions. Its fourteenth-century chapel is another of the three where the Catholic Mass has been celebrated without a break since the Reformation.

The ruined remains of Warblington Castle

Above: Hendred House: the East side with the chapel on the left.

Right: The south garden and chapel.

Stonor Park, with the chapel in the mid-right foreground.

The chapel contains sarsen and pudding stones which belong to a prehistoric past in the darkness before Domesday and indeed Stonor was an ancient house even before Henry VIII's marital difficulties threw the nation into crisis. The Stonor family had prospered under the Tudors, with Thomas Stonor (1450-1512) one of the four horsemen chosen to accompany the body of Henry VII at his state funeral.

Thomas's son, Sir Walter Stonor (1477-1550) remained loyal to the Pope but was a pragmatic man who did not parade his conscience. He rose steadily in Henry VIII's esteem to become Lieutenant of the Tower of London. Happily for Sir Walter he did not have to preside over the imprisonment of any of his relatives, and his good fortune saw him safely through the first three turbulent years of the brief reign of Edward VI. When Sir Walter died, he was still a member of the King's Commission for the Peace in Oxfordshire, a body charged with rooting out recusant papists.

Less fortunate, however, was Sir Walter's first cousin by marriage, Sir Adrian Fortesque. The two men fought out a long inheritance battle with Sir Adrian, who had lived at Stonor with his wife for many years, eventually forced to quit the house in favour of his rival, though he was compensated with the Stonor lands in Gloucestershire, Devon and Kent.

He and Sir Walter were very different characters. Sir Adrian was publicly disapproving of Henry VIII's break with Rome and struck out a reference in his missal to the king as supreme head of the Church in England. Arrested in August 1534 on suspicion of being 'evil in religion', he was held at Marshalsea Prison at Southwark in London. Although he was Anne Boleyn's first cousin, Sir Adrian could count on no help from the queen as the king grew increasingly disillusioned with his second wife. Like Anne, Sir Adrian was never tried. Instead he was condemned under the same Bill of Attainder used against Margaret Pole. Beheaded in July 1539, he was one of the earliest Catholic martyrs and was beatified – declared blessed – by the Pope in 1895.

Sir Walter was succeeded at Stonor by his nephew Francis who followed his uncle's example and lived quietly at the house throughout Queen Mary's reign. He died soon after Elizabeth, daughter of his distant relative, Anne Boleyn, came to the throne in 1558.

Francis's widow Lady Cecily Stonor, however, was made of more forthright stuff. Her uncle, the Carthusian monk and former royal favourite Sebastian Newdigate, had refused gifts of money and jewels from Henry VIII to renounce Rome and had been hung, drawn and quartered at Tyburn.

Lady Cecily decamped to Stonor Lodge and turned the main house into a refuge for a new generation of priests, the product of the seminary at Douai dedicated to turning out the foot soldiers who would win back 'Mary's Dowry', England, for the Pope. This secret army of Jesuits aroused extraordinary alarm in the Elizabethan court and society. It was treasonable to shelter any of them in your house.

Undeterred by such mortal considerations, Lady Cecily welcomed, under cover of night, a series of illicit tenants into Stonor. The most celebrated was the Oxford-educated Jesuit, Edmund Campion, author of the vade mecum of protestors in favour of religious toleration, the *Decem Rationes* or 'Ten Reasons'. Publishing such a tract in Elizabethan England was a risky business. A bookseller, William Carter, had already perished at Tyburn for printing Catholic literature. Stonor, under Campion's direction, housed a secret press which churned out copies in the early spring of 1581.

With the countryside awash with secret agents and informers, Campion and his fellow priests lived and worked in a secret hiding place high above Stonor's front porch known to its occupiers as Mount Pleasant. Should the house be searched and Mount Pleasant uncovered, another secret door led off it to a ladder which came out under the central gable of the roof. A makeshift chapel was hidden in the rafters.

The layout of this maze can only be guessed at by today's visitors. Stonor's architectural history, spanning back 800 years, is complex, with its impressive Georgian state rooms slotted into an untidy and much older shell, with unexplained nooks and crannies abounding. Any one of them might have housed Campion. In one bedroom in the West Wing, known as Little Attic, for instance, a panel of brickwork was discovered in 1964 to disguise a pivoting door leading to the gables. But experts are unclear as to whether this dates from Campion's time, or from later when Lady Cecily's descendants carried on her work of sheltering priests and made substantial alterations to the house to that end.

Six days after Campion left Stonor in July 1581 he was captured. He proved only human on the rack and soon was spilling Stonor's secrets. The Privy Council sent Sir Henry Neville to root out the colony of traitors to the Crown. Four printers, one priest, another visitor and Lady Cecily's younger son, John Stonor, were seized.

At his trial, Campion rediscovered his courage. 'In condemning us', he told his accusers, 'you condemn all your ancestors, all the ancient priests, bishops and kings, and all that was once the glory of England, the island of saints, and the most devoted child of the See of Saint Peter.' On the scaffold Campion begged forgiveness of all those he himself had betrayed to the authorities. Hung alongside him were two other priests, Alexander Bryant and Ralph Sherwin.

Sherwin, the last to die, paused before mounting the scaffold to kiss the hangman's hand, still dripping with Campion's blood. Such courage and faith led at least one member of the crowd, Henry Walpole, to convert on the spot. He trained as a Jesuit, like Campion, and was to suffer a similar fate.

Elizabeth could not stomach those whom she saw as a direct threat to her own survival and was merciless in her pursuit of the missionary priests. But with those who harboured them, she occasionally showed compassion. John Stonor spent only eight months in the Tower. In a turn of events that might have inspired Gilbert and Sullivan's *Yeoman of the Guard*, the Lieutenant's daughter fell in love with him, was converted and persuaded to carry messages between the Catholic prisoners there and at Marshalsea. On John's release, he went into exile and never saw Stonor – or his unhappy paramour – again.

Lady Cecily was treated leniently by the judges on account of her age and social standing. Though she accepted their largesse, it did not deter her from harbouring still more priests between 1586 and 1590 at Stonor. Caught in the act once again, she was sent to prison at 70 where, it is assumed, she died behind bars but unbroken.

Her heirs took up the mantle, in spite of the financial penalties and physical threats of the Crown. Cut off from the public life that had once sustained them, debarred from the universities and centres of learning, and forced like the wild geese to emigrate to find sustenance in a cold and unwelcoming climate, the Stonors clung like a limpet to the rock of faith despite bone-crunching blows that sought to prise them loose. Following Catholic Emancipation in 1829 they re-emerged and found a place at Queen Victoria's court where Thomas Stonor, who served as a Member of Parliament, was rewarded with a peerage.

His descendant the banker Lord Camoys continues to live at Stonor to this day and has worked hard to preserve this shrine of English Catholicism, with its serene brick façade and clutch of medieval buildings of flint, chalk and timber, in the face of a financial crisis which at one stage threatened its future. Alongside the scars of sorrow and persecution are the trophies of quieter times, of building, preserving and even, most English of all, gardening.

Stonor is open to the public.

Oxburgh Hall

NORFOLK

Virescit vulnere virtus
(Virtue flourishes by a wound)
*One of Mary Queen of Scots' favourite emblems,
as seen on her tapestries at Oxburgh*

Though Mary Queen of Scots never visited the Bedingfelds at their splendid fifteenth-century moated home in the heart of Norfolk, her embroidered green velvet hangings, completed by the ill-fated Catholic heir presumptive to Elizabeth's throne during her long years of captivity in England, are among the treasures of Oxburgh Hall. Brought to the house on her marriage to Sir Richard Bedingfeld in 1761 by Mary Browne, a descendant of one of the Catholic commissioners at Mary's trial, they are now part of the fabric of this great house, a centre of unreformed Catholicism throughout the persecutions.

Bedingfelds first arrived at Oxburgh in 1462 by a quirk of misfortune when the then owner, Sir Thomas Tuddenham, was executed for treason.

The property passed to his sister, Margaret, who had married Edmund Bedingfeld of Suffolk. In 1482 their grandson built the house with its defensive moat around a central courtyard and, with various additions and subtractions, Oxburgh remains true to that original design to this day.

The Bedingfelds became trusted royal servants under the Tudors. Henry VII visited Oxburgh in August 1497 and in 1529 Henry VIII appointed a subsequent Sir Edmund Bedingfeld Sheriff of Norfolk and Suffolk. Four years later the king placed his rejected queen, Catherine of Aragon, under Sir Edmund's watchful eye when he made him Steward and Comptroller of her household.

Catherine was effectively under house arrest at Kimbolton Castle and Sir Edmund endeavoured to carry out his duty loyally but with sensitivity towards the queen who died in 1536. His task was made all the more delicate by his own continuing Catholicism.

His son and heir, Sir Henry Bedingfeld, was one of the leading supporters of Mary Tudor, Catherine's daughter. When Edward VI died in 1553, there were attempts to exclude both Mary and her half-sister Elizabeth from the succession and put Lady Jane Grey on the throne. Confronted by these moves, Mary regrouped at Kenninghall in Norfolk where Sir Henry was among those who first rallied to her cause. He accompanied her on her triumphant march to London. His reward was to be appointed a Privy Counsellor and Governor of the Tower of London.

Though Mary had come to an agreement with Elizabeth, there was continuing mistrust between the two and, in March 1554, the young princess was imprisoned in the Tower of London which was placed in the charge of Sir Henry. He subsequently accompanied Elizabeth to Woodstock and later Hampton Court, always solicitous for her welfare but faithful in keeping her incommunicado as the queen had demanded.

Elizabeth's accession in 1558 might have been a moment for extracting vengeance on Sir Henry but though he lost all his crown appointments and retired to his estates, the new queen greeted at court her 'jaylor' as she referred to him and is reported to have remarked: 'If we have anie prisoner whom we would have hardlie and strictly kept, we will send him to you.'

Elizabeth though apparently bore Sir Henry no ill-will and as Catholics suffered increasingly during her reign, he was left relatively undisturbed. Indeed in 1578 she planned to visit Oxburgh but had to postpone. Only in the last years of her reign did Sir Henry suffer fines and the threat of imprisonment for his loyalty to Rome.

It was in this period that a priest-hole was constructed at Oxburgh to shelter visiting Catholic clergy from the prying eyes of the queen's pursuivants in a county that was for the most part fervently Protestant. The hide is in the main gatehouse and is entered via the King's Room, so named in memory of Henry VII's visit. In a closet in the northeast turret of the gatehouse is a recess where the tiled floor, if pressed in the right spot, swings back on a pivot to reveal a secret hiding place. The whole construction is believed to be the work of the most famous builder of priest-holes, Nicholas 'Little John' Owen.

The Bedingfelds saw their estates shrink and their coffers empty in the following years but never once considered abandoning their faith. They were given a baronetcy by Charles II in 1661 in lieu of the £47,000 they had lost supporting his father during the Civil War.

With the arrival of William and Mary in 1689 a new wave of anti-Catholicism was unleashed and the family – like other Catholics in this period – were forbidden from going further than five miles from their home. Their finances were rescued in the early eighteenth century by the marriage of Sir Henry Bedingfeld to the Protestant heiress Lady Elizabeth Boyle, known as

'Lady Betty'. Though it was undoubtedly a happy match – they had eight children – it had the added bonus of affording a degree of protection for Oxburgh from whatever penal measures were still enforced on Catholics.

It was their son Richard whose marriage to the Honourable Mary Browne, daughter of Viscount Montague of Cowdray in Sussex, brought Mary Queen of Scots' hangings to Oxburgh. Other panels worked by her are in the Victoria and Albert Museum, Hardwick Hall and Holyroodhouse in Edinburgh, but the bulk of her work is at Oxburgh.

The smaller panels depict emblems of birds, beasts and fish, taken from woodcuts in contemporary books of natural history. The Marian Panel shows in its centrepiece a curved pruning knife cutting out the unfruitful stem of a vine. In 1570 Mary had sent a cushion with this same design to the Duke of Norfolk who was plotting to marry her. It has been taken to suggest that the unfruitful or childless vine – Elizabeth – should be cut down and the flourishing branch – Mary – left to blossom.

Sir Richard's child, another Richard, who inherited in 1795, was the first Bedingfeld for many years to be educated in England. He was among the pupils of the newly-established Catholic college at Ware in Hertfordshire, later a seminary. His wife Charlotte was named a Lady-in-Waiting to Queen Adelaide, spouse of William IV, in 1830, a first sign that the Catholic Emancipation Act of the previous year was taking effect at court.

That same piece of legislation cleared the way in 1835 for the next baronet, another Sir Henry, to build a private Catholic chapel in the grounds of Oxburgh. Constructed of bricks from some Tudor cottages which Sir Henry had demolished, its design has been attributed to Augustus Welby Pugin. Its stained glass window features the seated figure of Saint John the Baptist while the magnificent triptych above the altar was made in Antwerp between 1510 and 1520.

In the nineteenth and twentieth centuries, the Bedingfelds have continued to flourish, counting among their number such eccentrics as the eighth baronet who became a cowboy in the Wild West of America and rode with Wild Bill Hickok, and the remarkable Sybil, Lady Bedingfeld who died in 1985 at the age of 102 and who in 1952 rescued the house after it had been sold and then passed it to the National Trust. It is now open to the public and popular with film-makers as a period setting. The current heir to the title, Henry Bedingfeld, York Herald, lives at Oxburgh with his family.

Broughton Hall

YORKSHIRE

Let two laymen, one a Roman Catholic, the other of the reformed religion, provided they are men of good judgement, knowing in controversy, and are not resolved to eavil before they meet...let I say, two such men fairly own what each of 'em believed and...I am certain...the difference between 'em will be the splitting of a hair.

Stephen Tempest 'Religio Laici'

THE long classical façade of Broughton Hall, framed by gentle hills, presents an appropriately proud face to the outside world, for the Tempest family, who have lived here since the fourteenth century, have never been afraid to stand up for their beliefs, no matter what the consequences, personal, social or financial.

One of their number, Robert Tempest, played a leading part in the Rising of the Northern Earls in 1569, an ill-organized attempt to install Mary Queen of Scots in place of Elizabeth. Though the Rising attracted little popular support in the nation as a whole, it became in Yorkshire and the northern counties a focus for a broad range of opposition to royal policies.

High on the list of grievances uniting the rebels was the Dissolution of the Monasteries. Henry VIII's brutal attack on the great Yorkshire monasteries of Fountains, Jervaulx and Sawley sparked the Pilgrimage of Grace in 1536 under Robert Aske and cost all three abbots their lives. Nicholas Tempest, from a junior branch of the family, was one of the leaders of the Pilgrimage and he was executed at Tyburn in 1537.

But the question of the monasteries continued to act as a focus for discontent. Like many others, high-born and low, Robert Tempest – again from a junior branch of this prolific and far-flung family – wanted to see a return to the monastic system that had been the mainstay of economic and spiritual life in his area. The Tempest family had long been closely associated with Fountains in particular as the surviving abbey records show.

Though the Rising spread rapidly, like a fire on the moorlands that surround Broughton, it was snuffed out just as quickly. Its leader, the Duke of Norfolk, was arrested before plans reached fruition and put in the Tower. On hearing of his fate, the local commanders, the Earls of Westmoreland and Northumberland, wanted to back out but were persuaded, reluctantly, to take up arms by popular pressure. Robert Tempest joined them along with his near neighbour and fellow Catholic, Thomas Markenfield of Markenfield Hall.

The massed ranks of the rebels began their campaign at Durham Cathedral where they made a bonfire out of Elizabethan prayer books. They marched on to Ripon for a blessing at the Minster but further south on their way to liberate Mary Queen of Scots the rebel army disintegrated at the first sign of engagement. Westmoreland and Northumberland fled to Scotland, though the latter was brought back and executed at York. Markenfield abandoned the family home for ever for the Continent whence he was followed by Robert Tempest who later trained for the priesthood.

Markenfield lay empty, the haunt of bats and owls. Broughton might well have suffered the same fate for, in addition to the involvement of Robert, the mistress of the house, Isabel Tempest, was a niece of the Earl of Northumberland, one of the ringleaders. Though she was repeatedly fined for her recusancy in the years that followed, the Tempests at Broughton survived the aftermath of the Rising in which 900 people were executed and 66 constables hanged for neglect of their duty to the Crown.

At the dawn of James I's reign in 1603, it briefly seemed that the worst of the persecutions were over. The new king even granted the head of the family, Stephen Tempest, a knighthood. Sir Stephen had been overseeing the rebuilding of the house, begun in 1597. This Elizabethan core remains at the heart of the present house.

However, darker days were to follow. Sir Stephen's son fought alongside the king in the Civil War and, as a consequence, Broughton was sequestrated in 1644. His brother Robert, a Captain of the Foot, is thought to have been killed by the Parliamentary forces on the lawn of Broughton in 1646.

Though the property was returned to the family with the Restoration, 1679 saw the next generation of Tempests embroiled in an alleged conspiracy to depose Charles II. Stephen Tempest was arrested, tried and acquitted for his part in the so-called Gascoigne Plot. His widowed aunt, Dame Anne Tempest, suffered a similar fate with the same outcome. The tapestry that she completed while in prison hangs at the foot of Broughton's stairwell today. A Jesuit priest charged alongside her, Thomas Thwing, was executed.

Stephen lived on through the ensuing period of anti-Catholic legislation under William and Mary and died in 1742 at the age of 88. His son, another Stephen, was something of a writer. His book *Religio Laici* – 'Religion for the Layman'- combined piety with the practical morality he felt the obligation of the squire class.

Denied posts in government or the military, various Tempests engaged sporadically in commerce. Though a distant branch of the family in the northeast were industrial pioneers, amassing a substantial fortune through coal-mining and involvement in various canal projects, the Broughton Tempests made no great impact in the the world of industry and business.

Marriage benefited the family coffers and work was begun, around 1750, on rebuilding Broughton as a three-storey mansion of smooth golden ashlar. The façade of Broughton was given an eccentric flourish in the nineteenth century with the addition of a decorative porte-cochere. The Gothic chapel is richly stencilled and has recently been restored.

In 1836 the family bought a plot of land in neighbouring Skipton and there built the parish church of Saint Stephen's which incorporates a private Tempest vault.

Broughton remains the family home. Henry Tempest, the current owner, succeeded his brother Stephen in 1970 and has continued a tradition of Tempest squires in this area of Yorkshire which stretches back for 29 generations.

Norbury Manor

DERBYSHIRE

When Garlick did the ladder kiss,
And Sympson after hie,
Me thought that there Saint Andrew was,
Desirous for to die.

When Ludlam looked on smilingly,
And joyful did remain,
It seemed Saint Stephen was standing by,
For to be stoned again
Bishop Richard Challoner

Norbury Manor is a like a Russian doll. Peel off one layer and you uncover another and another and another concealed within. The pretty Restoration façade hides a Tudor house which includes a medieval wing which replaced an earlier timber building. And Norbury's history is no less labyrinthine. Amid tales of great heroism in defence of the Pope, it has also witnessed episodes of unexpected treachery and times of trimming.

Home to various branches of the Fitzherbert family from 1125 until modern times, Norbury stands alongside its fourteenth-century church, dominated by the tomb of Nicholas Fitzherbert, magnificent with its alabaster figure dressed in plate armour and topped with the family crest, a clenched left hand within a gauntlet.

The Fitzherberts were one of the great recusant families and, aside from the Norbury branch, counted among their number Father Thomas Fitzherbert, Rector of the English College in Rome in the darkest days of persecutions, and – by marriage – Maria Fitzherbert, the Catholic widow whose secret wedding to the future George IV in 1785 threatened a constitutional crisis.

Nicholas Fitzherbert acquired the freehold of Norbury in 1448 and passed it on to a succession of colourful and often single-minded men like John Fitzherbert, thirteenth Lord of Norbury in the immediate pre-Reformation period. He wrote a seminal work on husbandry. Among his pearls of wisdom was his classification of the ten properties of a woman – which follows his ten properties of an ass. John's perfect mate would have a broad forehead, wide buttocks and be 'easye to lepe vppon...well sturrynge vnder a man...(and)...ever to be chowynge on the brydell'.

Such was the unusual mix in the Fitzherbert genes that the next master of Norbury, John's brother Sir Antony, was a deeply religious intellectual who was a leading lawyer in Henry VIII's reign. His *Grand Abridgement of the Common Law*, printed in 1514, was one of the earliest attempts at codification. He prospered under Henry, rising to be Justice of Common Pleas. However, his unrepentant Catholicism, though it did not bring him any physical hardship, is thought to have blocked his passage to the coveted post of Lord Chief Justice which many felt was his by rights.

Sir Antony indeed found himself caught between his desire to serve his king well and his conscience. With the suppression of the monasteries, he was called upon to take possession of several abbeys. This he did with a heavy heart. He sat on the tribunals that tried and convicted the martyrs,

Above: The *parterre* or knot garden

Below: Oxburgh Hall.

Above: Broughton Hall from the river.

Below: A rear view with the chapel on the far left.

Above: Norbury Manor: the medieval chapel
and herb garden

Left: Inside the chapel.

The rear elevation of Baddesley Clinton.

Richard Reynolds and John Hale and more notably Thomas More and John Fisher. Sir Anthony refused, however, to benefit personally from seized lands and was reputed to be the only man who dared rebuke the king for the excesses of his alienation of church property and live to tell the tale.

If later generations judged him a compromised character, Sir Antony himself left such matters up to God. In the guest bedroom, visitors can still read the religious quotations that he had inscribed on the oak panels. 'We shall all stand before the judgement of Christ...each one of us shall render account of himself to God'. And on his deathbed in 1538, Sir Antony solemnly enjoined his children not to accept grants of monastic lands from the monarch.

This last wish his heir, Sir Thomas Fitzherbert, respected, though he followed in his father's footsteps in balancing faith with practical service to his sovereign. During the reign of Edward VI, he was appointed as one of the commissioners who compiled an inventory of church goods so that they might be sold to maximum profit.

He married the daughter and heiress of another Derbyshire landowner, Sir Arthur Eyre, and thus united Norbury and the adjoining estate of Over Padley. A stained-glass window, with the Fitzherbert and Eyre arms impaled, recalls their union.

By the time Queen Elizabeth came to the throne and outlawed 'papist' services, Sir Thomas had hardened in his religious convictions. He remained steadfast and unrepentant in his Mass attendance. As a result he was one of the earliest victims of the Elizabethan persecutions, locked up in the Fleet prison in London in 1561 along with fellow recusants the Bishop of Chester and the Dean of Saint Paul's.

To effect his release, he had to agree to attend a Protestant service, but he refused repeatedly to the bafflement of those who sought to save him from his fate. In 1563, the Bishop of London complained to a friend: 'Sir Thomas Fitzherbert is a very stiff man. We had a solemn assembly of commissioners only for his case, when Mr Chancellor of the Duchy was present, and they concluded to let Mr Fitzherbert be abroad upon sureties, if he would be bound in the meantime to go orderly to the church, without binding him to receive the Communion. That Sir Thomas refused.'

For 30 years, he went on refusing, confined to prison with all too brief periods of liberty, losing two-thirds of his lands in fines, and dying, poorer in material goods but still defiant in spirit, at the age of 74. His brother John Fitzherbert was also jailed on account of his unreformed faith and died in the Fleet prison in 1590, the year before Sir Thomas. Nothing could break their resolve. Even the imprisonment of John's son and Sir Thomas's nephew and heir, another Thomas, did not cause them to waver.

Sadly the young Fitzherbert was not made of such stern stuff. Given his already weak character, it was a tragic turn of events that threw him together, in Derby Gaol in 1583, with the arch pursuivant – or priest-hunter – Richard Topcliffe. Stuck in a prison that by Topcliffe's own admission 'always stank and bred corruption', Thomas recanted.

Not content with conforming to the new religion, he entered into a bond with Topcliffe to pay the latter £3,000 if the priest-hunter would persecute to death Sir Thomas and John Fitzherbert. Topcliffe had, it seems, persuaded his prey that the only way to inherit Norbury intact was to betray his nearest and dearest before they frittered it away paying fines. What is more Topcliffe had his eye on Padley – 'a delightful and solitary place' he once called it – as a retirement home.

The dastardly scheme failed to succeed by virtue of that traditional Fitzherbert loyalty to the Crown in matters temporal. Sir Thomas, what-ever his reticence on the new religion, never ceased to express his bond to the queen and, when the Spanish Armada loomed, volunteered to pay double the tax imposed on his estate as his contribution in a national emergency. Topcliffe therefore had trouble presenting his quarry as a traitor, though he had him transferred to the Tower of London.

Sir Thomas's noble defiance, however, seemed only to push the family Judas, young Thomas, to baser betrayal. He informed on other relatives for sheltering Catholic priests at Padley. Two members of the Jesuit mission, Fathers Nicholas Garlick and Robert Ludlam, were discovered hiding in a chimney in the house on July 12, 1588, taken to Derby Gaol and hung, drawn and quartered along with Father Richard Sympson.

All three – later celebrated in Bishop Challoner's ode – fell victim to a wave of hysteria in the summer of 1588, triggered by the approach of the Armada, sent by the Spanish king to reconvert Protestant England. Some 21 priests, nine laymen and one woman were executed in those three months as the authorities attempted to discourage anyone thinking of giving succour to the invaders. In the end the weather did the job for them, knocking the Armada off course with a little help from Sir Francis Drake.

Despairing of young Thomas's ability to deliver sufficient evidence to damn his uncle, Topcliffe turned to torturing Sir Thomas's servants to try to build a sufficient case against their master to get him condemned to death. Alice Rolston, housekeeper at Norbury, and Thomas Coxson, keeper of Sir Thomas's lands at Ridway, both suffered in the process.

With Sir Thomas's death in 1591, his nephew finally inherited Norbury and Topcliffe seized Padley. A last gasp attempt by Sir Thomas to change the succession failed when Topcliffe found the new will in his cell and had it destroyed.

Neither conspirator lived long though to enjoy their ill-gotten gains. Young Fitzherbert descended into petty crime and died without issue.

Topcliffe was universally reviled and few mourned his passing in 1604.

Norbury went to another of the venerable Sir Thomas's nephews, Sir John Fitzherbert, the last of the family to inherit the house in the direct male line. He fought on the Royalist side in the Civil War and died in 1649, the same year as the king whom he had so loyally served was executed.

Norbury passed to cousins who lived nearby in some style at Swynnerton Park and it fell into disuse. Financial difficulties forced the family to sell both properties, now in a sad state of disrepair, in the nineteenth century. An eccentric kinsman of the Fitzherberts, Marcus Stapleton Martin, rescued Norbury this century and passed it to the National Trust in the 1980s. The house is now occupied by his cousin Charles Wright, a senior member of the Catholic Knights of Malta.

BADDESLEY CLINTON

WARWICKSHIRE

O worn grey stones, that yet are splashed with red
As though with martyrs' blood, a lesson high
Ye teach, of worldly glories long since dead,
And of the faith of Christ that cannot die.

Dom Bede Camm

CARDINAL John Henry Newman, the eminent Victorian whose conversion to Rome gave English Catholicism its first flush of post-Reformation respectability, sketched in 1852 the then prevailing impression of national Catholic life. It was characterized, he said, by 'an old-fashioned house of gloomy appearance, closed in with high walls, with an iron gate...and the report attaching to it that "Roman Catholics" lived there; but who they were, or what they did...no one could tell, though it had an unpleasant sound'.

With its austere entrance front of grey stone, the ancient moated manor house of Baddesley Clinton at first glimpse slots neatly into Newman's description. Yet this fifteenth-century hall, owned by the staunchly

Catholic Ferrers family for eleven generations father-to-son, has on closer inspection an impossibly romantic past, with its priest-holes, its martyrs and its two brave and indomitable mistresses.

Baddesley Clinton's foundations were probably laid by a Saxon called Baeddi who gave the estate its name when he made his home in a ley in the Forest of Arden. One part of the estate, Hay Wood, remains uncleared – the last surviving fragment of the untamed forest.

While Henry VIII was busy making his break from Rome, Baddesley slumbered undisturbed. Turbulent times were to come though. Its squire throughout the subsequent reigns of Edward, Mary, Elizabeth and James I was Henry Ferrers. Known as 'The Antiquary', he was less concerned with matters of religion – though he stayed true to Rome – than with remodelling his house with the panelling and carved chimneypieces seen today, and the armorial glass that is so much a feature of Baddesley.

Ferrers's taste for home improvements, however, emptied the family coffers and in the 1590s he found himself in a London debtors' jail. In the hope of furnishing his eventual release, he let Baddesley to Anne Vaux and her widowed sister, Eleanor Brookesby, daughters of Lord Vaux of Harrowden, an unrepentant Catholic. While for Ferrers discretion was the better part of valour, the new mistresses of Baddesley defied the laws of the land to shelter Jesuit priests under their roof.

They did not escape the notice of government spies and on October 19, 1591, the house was searched following a tip-off. The Jesuit John Gerard, then hiding at Baddesley, was attending a secret Mass when the pursuivants or priest-hunters arrived. He describes what happened in his autobiography:

Father Southwell heard the din. He guessed what it was all about and slipped off his vestments and stripped the altar bare. While he was doing this, we laid hold of all our personal belongings: nothing was left to betray the presence of a priest. Even our boots and swords were hidden away – they would have roused suspicions if none of the people they were to belong to were to be found. Our beds presented a problem as they were still warm and merely covered in the usual way preparatory to being made. Some of us went off and turned the beds and put the cold side up to delude anyone who put his hand in to feel them.

For four hours Southwell, Gerard and his brothers in faith cowered in a priest-hole, below ground level in this moated house and therefore flooded with water up to their ankles. But their tormentors could not unearth them and were put off the trail by Anne Vaux who made a fine display of aristocratic indignation before relenting and offering the intruders a hearty breakfast to see them on their way. 'All they did', wrote Gerard, 'was to show how dogged and spiteful they could be, and how forbearing Catholics were. Yes, that is the pitiful lot of Catholics.'

Three of the priests who sheltered in Baddesley that night died martyrs. First to be captured was Father Robert Southwell, the poet of Warblington, who was tortured by Richard Topcliffe. Despite pleas to Elizabeth for clemency and the good offices of the Countess of Arundel who sent him clean linen when he was held in the Tower, he was executed at the age of 33 in February 1595. In the aftermath of the Gunpowder Plot, Father Edward Oldcorne – April 1606 – and Father Henry Garnet – May of the same year – followed Southwell to the scaffold where they were hanged until semi-conscious, then cut down, disembowelled, castrated and dismembered. According to Gerard, Oldcorne's intestines burned for fourteen days which was taken by some to be a miracle, albeit a gruesome one.

The active career of the missionary priests was a short one and Topcliffe was proud of his knack of keeping it that way. In a letter to Elizabeth, he crowed: 'I have helped more traitors (to Tyburn) than all the noblemen and gentlemen of your court, your counsellors excepted'. Gerard too was among his victims, but he escaped with his life.

The hiding hole at Baddesley that Gerard describes can be viewed today from the house's kitchen. It was entered via the present sacristy, down the former garderobe flue. Another hiding place was only uncovered in 1935 and is situated above the gatehouse. This lath-and-plaster hutch in the roof above a closet is reputed to have been used by Eleanor Brookesby while her sister was giving the pursuivants their marching orders. A third runs under the gable and was said to have been built for Father Thomas Lister, a close associate of Oldcorne, who found the other shelters too claustrophobic.

All three places are thought to be the work of Garnet's diminutive servant, Nicholas Owen, better known as Little John. He was, Gerard writes, 'well-known as the chief designer and builder of hiding places in England', and was later captured at Coughton Court.

The descendants of Henry Ferrers clung on to their family home despite the financial mess he bequeathed them. True to Newman's description, they retreated behind closed gates and high walls and sat out the remaining years of persecution for those loyal to the Pope.

In the 1850s, soon after the restoration of the Catholic hierarchy in England and Wales, the house enjoyed a new lease of life under Marmion and Rebecca Ferrers and the latter's aunt, Lady Chatterton and her second husband, Heneage. This eccentric quartet replenished the hall with such 'Catholic' memorabilia as a bed saved from the wreck of one of the ships in the Spanish Armada. They laid out the courtyard garden and gave what had become a bleak house an air of romantic if unworldly charm.

Marmion's great-nephew was forced to sell the house in 1940 and it has since been acquired by the National Trust. The impoverishment of successive generations of Ferrerses means that unlike many English country houses it retains its historic character to an unusual degree. The spirit of the house is summed up by the motto in Baddesley Clinton's chapel: 'Transit Gloria Mundi/Fides Catholica Manet' (Worldly glory is transitory, but the Catholic faith endures).

Hoghton Tower

LANCASHIRE

At Hoghton high which was a bower
Of sports and lordly pleasure
I wept: and left that lofty tower
Which was my chiefest treasure.
To save my soul and lose the rest
It was my true pretence;
Like frightened bird I left my nest
To keep my conscience

From 'The Blessed Conscience'
attributed to Roger Anderson

Hoghton Tower with its battlements and gateways stands on a ridge southeast of Preston, as strong and aloof as the man who built it there in 1565. Thomas Hoghton was an unreformed Catholic and his house, like its squire, was out of tune with the Elizabethan period. Dark, isolated and romantic, from a distance it looks like a fortified town of medieval England.

The Hoghton family had owned the surrounding lands since the Norman Conquest, but neither their ancient name, their wealth nor their fortress could protect them from the winds of change sweeping England in the sixteenth century.

Thomas Hoghton was closely associated with his Lancastrian neighbour, William Allen, who, though a Canon of York at the time of Elizabeth's accession, quickly fell out of favour with the queen on account of his insistence that attending services of the Established Church was a sin. Allen resigned as Principal and Proctor of St Mary's Hall, Oxford, rather than take the Oath of Supremacy and in 1561 went into exile at Louvain.

He returned periodically to England to bolster the Catholic cause and was present at celebrations to mark the rebuilding of Hoghton Tower in 1565. Three years later he established his base on the Continent when he founded a seminary at Douai, dedicated to training priests who would bring England back to the papal fold. Made a cardinal by Rome to reward him for his fidelity, Allen included among his students Thomas Hoghton's son, also called Thomas.

Hoghton senior had travelled with his neighbour into exile in 1569, the year of the failure of the Northern Rising. He thus avoided the bloody persecution that followed its collapse.

Thomas Hoghton senior took with him his loyal butler, Roger Anderson. Among the framed papers at Hoghton Tower today is a set of manuscript verses entitled 'The Blessed Conscience'. Attributed to Anderson, they describe his master's grief at abandoning the home he had lovingly built.

Fair England, now ten times adieu,
and friends that therin dwell;
Farewell, my brother Richard true
Whom I did love so well.
Farewell, farewell, good people all,
And learn experience:

Love not too much the golden ball
But keep your conscience.

Richard Hoghton, the 'brother true' referred to in the verse, obtained permission in 1576 from the queen herself to visit his brother on the Continent. Her hopes of encouraging his return from exile proved ill-founded, as she later discovered when she tried to persuade Thomas herself. He died in 1580 without ever seeing England again.

Soon after his death Hoghton Tower was visited by none other than Father Edmund Campion SJ, a family friend whose publishing exploits we have already read of in connection with Stonor. The most wanted man in England showed why the authorities considered him such a threat when he preached in Hoghton's chapel and attracted a crowd that contained many of the leading families of Lancashire. His triumph is recorded in a popular song of the period, extolling his virtues.

The Tower had never man
that stood in more defense,
More farre from foile, more full of fayth
or more sensere of sence

When Campion was later arrested and broken under torture, he may have mentioned his time at Hoghton for a letter from the Privy Council, dated August 2, 1581, orders Sir John Byron, Sheriff of Lancashire, to search houses thought to have harboured the Jesuit priest 'and especially the house of Richard Hoghton where, it is said, the said Campion left his books'. In the ensuing raid, a number of papers were seized.

Like Campion, Thomas Hoghton junior was to die for his faith. After his ordination at Douai, he returned to his native Lancashire, an area where loyalty to the Pope was slow to be replaced by fidelity to the monarch. He ministered to the recusant families but was captured and thrown into Salford Gaol. He is believed to have died there in 1584.

Mysteriously three hundred years later an old chest was found in a hollow not far from Hoghton. It contained candlesticks and 'old wooden images', thought to have come from the Tower's chapel and been hidden to avoid the attentions of the pursuivants.

One reason why they were left unclaimed was that Thomas's heir, his nephew Richard Hoghton, was a Protestant. As was the fate of other Catholic heirs in this period of persecution, he was taken away from his family to be raised in the new religion. He was 'fostered' by Sir Gilbert Gerard, Master of the Rolls and a man loyal to the Crown in matters of religion, and later married off to Katherine, one of Gerard's daughters.

Elevated to the baronetcy by James I in 1611, Sir Richard, by a bitter irony, became a noted priest-hunter. In 1600 he arrested two priests who were later executed in Lancaster. As a mark of royal approval, Sir Richard played host in April 1617 to the king and the Duke of Buckingham at Hoghton Tower. The Banqueting Hall, which is two storeys high and fills the north range, contains to this day the Jacobean table where the king dined and is reputed to have knighted the Sir-Loin of beef. The original bill of fare, known as the Lord's Diet, from this royal evening is also on display.

The Hoghton family remained Protestant for many generations, providing Members of Parliament for Preston throughout the eighteenth century. In this period the family moved out of Hoghton and it fell into disrepair, but restoration was begun in the 1860s by Sir Henry de Hoghton who added the 'de' as a sign of the antiquarian enthusiasm that made him move back to the ancestral seat.

The present incumbent Sir Richard Bernard Cuthbert de Hoghton was educated at the Benedictine school of Ampleforth. He is a Knight of Malta and Deputy Lieutenant of Lancashire.

PLOTS, PENALTIES AND PERSECUTION

Mapledurham House

OXFORDSHIRE

She went to plain work and to purling brooks,
Old fashion'd halls, dull aunts and croaking rooks,
She went from Op'ra, park, assembly and play
To morning walks and pray'rs three hours a day
'On her leaving the Town after the Coronation'
by Alexander Pope for Martha Blount

THE Catholic martyrs of Elizabethan times were executed, in the authorities' eyes at least, in an effort to dissuade others from rejecting the National Church and the queen's supremacy in matters of religion. But their deaths sometimes had precisely the opposite effect. Sir Michael Blount, master of Mapledurham, was Lieutenant of the Tower of London between 1590 and 1595 and was so moved by the witness of two of the condemned men in his charge, Father Robert Southwell and Philip Howard, the Earl of Arundel, that he became ever more wedded to his Catholicism.

Sir Michael had prospered in the Elizabethan age. A former Sheriff of Oxfordshire and Member of Parliament, he raised a loan of £1,500 – around

£150,000 in today's money – to build himself a new home at Mapledurham, beside the Thames outside Caversham. It was erected alongside an existing manor house on this riverside site and today stands largely unaltered, a graceful Elizabethan hall of diapered brickwork, high gables and tall chimneys, built in the shape of the letter H.

Mapledurham is believed to be the only house built in the period of the persecutions with the intention of providing a secret refuge for Catholic priests as part of its design. Its priest-holes appear to have been integral to the original plan, not a later alteration as in other houses. Mapledurham's isolated location was an additional bonus for any such scheme, at the end of a long riverside track whose name, Chalk Pudding Lane, gives a clue to the fact it was often flooded and impassable.

Sir Michael would travel by river from the Tower to Mapledurham – an early example of commuting. A court favourite, his high standing with the queen saved him from being put on the spot over religion and he is thought never to have been asked to take the Oath of Supremacy. What resolve he had to stick to his Catholicism was undoubtedly strengthened by his contact with the Jesuit poet Southwell – whom Sir Michael called 'that saint' – and Howard. The earl died in the Tower seven weeks before Sir Michael's term of office came to an end. The Lieutenant reportedly went to Howard's deathbed and begged his forgiveness. The earl replied that 'God, who with His finger turneth the unstable wheel of this variable world, can in the revolution of a few days bring you to be a prisoner also, and to be kept in the same place where now you keep others'.

Sir Michael is indeed buried in the Tower's chapel, but with full honours in his capacity as a former Lieutenant. In effect he led a double life, maintaining both his loyalty at court in everything but religion, and simultaneously his own chaplain at Mapledurham.

Documentary evidence of the sheltering of priests at the house is thin on the ground. Usually such activity is recorded in the accounts of the trials either of captured Jesuits or of the host family. But the Blounts of Mapledurham escaped discovery. Nevertheless there were, it is thought, once six hiding places in the house, of which only two remain to this day. It was a centre for the Thames Valley area and the oyster shells, set in a triangle on the gable end facing the Thames, were a sign to passing Catholics that this was a recusant house.

Mapledurham was not finished until 1612, two years after Sir Michael's death. His son and heir, Richard, completed the work. He died in 1628 and is buried alongside his wife Cecily in what has traditionally been regarded as the 'family aisle' in Saint Margaret's which stands behind the house in the village of Mapledurham. This area, sectioned off from the main body of worshippers, was long believed to have allowed the Blounts to conform ostensibly to the 'new' religion each Sunday while keeping their conscience in the privacy of their own pews.

The story does not, however, stand up to scrutiny. For one thing the family maintained its own chapel in the gables of Mapledurham. And it was only in the later part of the nineteenth century, after a long-running case in the diocesan courts which ended up before the House of Lords, that their ownership of the Bardolf Aisle in Saint Margaret's was finally established.

Richard's heir, Sir Charles Blount, took up the Royalist cause with enthusiasm during the Civil War and was Scout Master General in the king's army. It was an allegiance that almost brought the family to ruin. When the Parliamentary forces under the Earl of Essex besieged Reading in April 1643, they sent a detachment to the noted Royalist stronghold of Mapledurham, four miles to the northwest. Essex's troops quickly overran the house and pillaged its goods. Not that there was much to take because

Sir Charles – whose portrait hangs in the entrance hall – was not much luckier with money than he was on the field of battle. In 1637 he had been forced to sell most of the contents of the house to clear his debts.

In the eighteenth century Mapledurham played host on many occasions to the Catholic poet Alexander Pope. His family had moved in the 1700s to nearby Binfield where their neighbour was Martha Englefield who later married and became Mrs Blount. Her daughters, Teresa and Martha, subsequently grew close to Alexander Pope. Many of Pope's writings which are kept at Mapledurham are in the form of letters to Mrs Blount from the young poet thanking her for her hospitality.

At Mapledurham, Pope found an environment where neither his Catholicism nor his physical disabilities set him apart and he grew close to the two sisters. At first it was Teresa – also called Zephelinda – who attracted his attention, though later Martha – or Parthenia – replaced her in the poet's affections. In October 1714, Martha was prevented from witnessing the coronation of George I when she was struck down by smallpox while in London. So Pope composed a poem 'On her leaving the Town after the Coronation' to cheer her up.

Pope too is believed to have played a part in the remodelling of Mapledurham's gardens around this period. The enclosed Elizabethan garden was swept away in a vast landscaping scheme, one of the first under-taken in England, which restored the natural beauty of the land going down to and along the Thames towards the Chiltern Hills. The use of statues was highly unusual for the time.

With the passage of the Second Relief Act in 1791, Michael Blount III felt able to build a chapel at the back of the house in Strawberry Hill Gothic style. His motivation was chiefly to provide a place of worship for Catholic émigrés who had fled the French Revolution and settled in substantial

Hoghton Tower from the main courtyard.

The east front of
Mapledurham House.

The rear of Coughton Court.

Above: Wardour Castle: the main house and the chapel from the north.

Below: The Chapel

Boscobel House over the courtyard.

Right: The courtyard.

Below: Wardley Hall: the garden (south) side.

Traquair House.

Right: A detail of the Bear Gates.

numbers in the Reading area. The new chapel, still used today, is believed to be the first, Catholic, legal, purpose-built one of its kind erected in England after the Reformation.

In the nineteenth century the Blounts once again took their place in public life. The mistress of the house founded a Catholic school in the village in the 1830s while in the 1880s a Blount, like his ancestors before him, was named High Sheriff of Oxfordshire.

The direct male line of Blounts died out in 1908 with John Darell Blount who had let the house out to tenants. It passed eventually to the Blounts' Eyston cousins of Hendred House and has now been lovingly restored. Mapledurham's Thames-side location has been suggested as the inspiration behind Toad Hall in Kenneth Graham's *Wind in the Willows*, but its next-door neighbour, Hardwick House, is thought a more likely candidate.

Mapledurham's picture postcard setting makes it one of the most attractive of the recusant houses. Some, however, find the quintessential Englishness of the location too much. 'There is even a water mill' Pevesner wrote, 'exactly where it should be. The whole place, one feels, is over-acting like mad.'

COUGHTON COURT

WARWICKSHIRE

Remember, remember, the fifth of November
Gunpowder, treason and plot
Popular ditty

Coughton Court, home to the Throckmorton family for over four hundred years, is little changed since the time of Henry VIII. As you approach Coughton's West Front you come face to face with Tudor England in all its grandeur and drama, but as you wander through the panelled rooms with their priest-holes and Catholic relics it is not the persecutions of Henry or Elizabeth that you remember. Rather it is the whisper of treachery and the murderous attempt against the lives of James I and the magnates who sat in his Parliament.

When James came to the throne in 1603, Catholics had hoped that he might treat them a little more kindly than Elizabeth. He had after all lent a sympathetic ear to their pleas for relief while king of Scotland. James, however, inherited from his predecessor Robert Cecil as chief minister and he oversaw the passage of ever more draconian legislation. In despair, many English Catholics grew bitter at the new impositions which became, in the words of the Jesuit John Gerard, 'the spurs' that pushed the Gunpowder Plotters 'upon that furious and fiery course which they afterwards fell into'.

Coughton was one of the centres of the conspiracy because it was well-known to many of the plotters. Its owner Thomas Throckmorton prudently went to stay elsewhere. (Present thinking suggests it was to Weston Underwood, another Throckmorton property.) Francis Tresham, who had grown up at Coughton, Sir Everad Digby, its current tenant and Robert Catesby, whose mother was a Throckmorton, were pivotal figures. Their intention was to mine under the throne and then, on the occasion of the opening of Parliament, blow up the king and his nobles all in one go. Guy Fawkes, an experienced sapper, was recruited to assist the gentlemen conspirators.

Digby spread the news of the plot among the Catholic gentry and arranged for them to assemble at the Lion Inn at Dunchurch on November 5, ostensibly for a hunting party, but in fact so that, on hearing that the fuse had been ignited, they could proceed to Combe and seize the king's daughter Elizabeth. At Coughton itself was gathered a party many of whose names have been mentioned already – Anne Vaux and Eleanor Brookesby, cousins of the Throckmortons, from nearby Baddesley Clinton; the priest-hole builder Nicholas 'Little John' Owen and the Jesuit Father Garnet. Also present were Lady Digby and another Jesuit, Father Tesimond.

The authorities later claimed that the women and priests prayed together for success in a chapel in the tower of Coughton, all the time glancing out of its windows lest danger be approaching. In the hiding place beneath the chapel room they sheltered waiting for news. When it came it was of a disaster. An anonymous warning sent to Lord Mounteagle had been passed on to Cecil. 'They would have blown up the Parliament House', Garnet told Tesimond, 'and were discovered and we are all utterly undone.'

Digby, Tresham and Father Garnet were among those arrested as conspirators although the available evidence suggests that Garnet had no foreknowledge of the plot. His protests of innocence were ignored and he suffered the prolonged torment of a traitor's death. Owen was subjected to special torture since, as already mentioned, he was the most prolific builder of priest-holes up and down the country. His captors believed he could reveal much of the underground Catholic network but, despite terrible suffering, he remained silent until his death under torture.

After the executions came the grasping for plunder. Ironically there was another Throckmorton, Sir Arthur, involved in this exercise. Sir Arthur's father, Sir Nicholas Throckmorton, recalls an earlier period when Coughton had been embroiled in affairs of state.

Sir Nicholas was the younger son of Sir George Throckmorton, the builder of Coughton Court, who had helped Henry VIII put down the Pilgrimage of Grace in 1536 but who was nevertheless a devout Catholic. On his death Coughton passed to Sir Robert Throckmorton who chose to eschew politics in favour of tending his estate. But his brother Sir Nicholas, who obtained his title from the Protestant Edward VI and took up the 'new' religion, felt no such restraint. Jailed during the reign of Queen Mary, he went on to be a confidant of Elizabeth.

Their relationship, however, grew strained. First Sir Nicholas's daughter Bessie married Sir Walter Raleigh much to the queen's fury. And then when Sir Nicholas was sent as a royal emissary to Mary Queen of Scots, he became close to the Catholic heir apparent. Though never convicted of plotting against Elizabeth, he was regarded with suspicion by the Earl of Leicester and is reputed to have been poisoned by him.

The shift Mary is supposed to have worn on the day of her execution in 1587 is kept at Coughton in the Tribune which adjoins the Dining Room. There is also a portrait of her dear friend, Sir Nicholas Throckmorton.

Like Sir Nicholas another Throckmorton, his Catholic cousin Francis, was touched by the intrigues around Mary Queen of Scots. However, Francis Throckmorton was a supporter without reserve and his plot to replace Elizabeth with Mary was uncovered by the queen's spymaster, Sir Francis Walsingham. Tortured on the rack, he eventually confessed. 'Now', he moaned, 'I have disclosed the secrets of her (Mary) who was the dearest thing to me in the world.' As he crawled away from the rack he murmured 'Chi a perso la fede, a perso l'onore' – 'Faith broken, honour lost'.

Though Sir Nicholas's brother and Francis's cousin Sir Robert avoided court and politics, he did allow Coughton to be used as a centre for the secret Jesuit mission to England. His son Thomas, the next lord of Coughton, spent 16 years in prison for his faith and suffered heavy fines, though he had left his home rather than get involved in the 1605 conspiracy. And Sir Robert's daughter Mary – who was mistress of Coughton when her brother was in jail – had married one of Francis Throckmorton's co-conspirators, Edward Arden.

Despite the involvement of their home in the Gunpowder Plot, the Throckmortons managed to hold on to Coughton. During the Civil War, the family sided with Charles I. Coughton was bombarded by the Roundheads and in October 1643 was occupied by a Parliamentary garrison from Warwick. They stayed for three months, leaving only when they had set fire to the house in three places.

Following the king's defeat Coughton was sequestrated but returned to the Throckmortons in 1651. As part of the restoration works, a new chapel was being built during James II's reign when Catholics once more felt confident enough to proclaim their beliefs in public. The 'Glorious Revolution', however, brought a mob to Coughton on 'Running Thursday', December 3, 1688, and they sacked the chapel. A century later the ruins were removed and used to fill in the moat.

In the following century the Throckmortons were among the instigators of attempts to reach a settlement between the recusant families and the Crown. The fifth baronet, Sir John Throckmorton, helped form the Cisalpine Club in the 1780s which recognized the Pope but advocated English bishops elected in England. And his nephew Sir Robert George Throckmorton was the first Catholic after the 1829 Emancipation Act to take the Oath of Allegiance and sit in the House of Commons. He built a Catholic parish church for Coughton.

Coughton was given to the National Trust after the Second World War by Lilian, Lady Throckmorton, mother of the penultimate baronet, Sir Robert. However, in accordance with a High Court order, a three hundred year lease was awarded back to the family. Her granddaughter, Clare McLaren-Throckmorton QC, who lives in the house, has overseen the transfer of some of the most historically important contents to the Trust. Among these is a picture which hangs in the Tower Room, dated 1596. It captures the spirit of the Throckmortons with the heads of the kings and queens of England from William Rufus to Elizabeth depicted above the arms of all the Catholic gentry who were imprisoned for recusancy.

Wardour Castle

WILTSHIRE

How vainly should that beggar chide his fate
Who quits his dunghill for a chair of state:
So fare it with us, when God doth displace
The gifts of fortune for the gifts of grace.
Written by the third Lord Arundell
while in the Tower in 1678

WITH its Palladian elegance and measured proportions, Wardour Castle has long been regarded as one of the finest eighteenth-century mansions in the country. Its circular, central staircase, topped by a dome and the pivot of the whole house, is an architectural gem. But Wardour's claim to a place in history rests on more than its good looks. For 400 years, starting in the reign of Henry VIII, the Catholic Arundell family lived in this corner of Wiltshire and their home during the years of persecution was the scene of many a dramatic and bloody event.

And none was more momentous than the siege of Wardour in 1643 during the Civil War. The Arundells, like most of the old Catholic families, sided with the Royalist forces of Charles I against the Puritan leadership of the Parliamentarians. The second Lord Arundell died in May 1643 of wounds received while fighting for the king at the Battle of Reading the previous month.

As he lay on his deathbed and with Royalist strongholds falling all over the south and west, his wife Lady Blanche was ordered to surrender Wardour Castle to the Parliamentary forces. A doughty descendant of Margaret Pole of Warblington, she refused. 'I know no Parliamentary army,' she responded. 'Troops of rebels are there in the field, enemies alike to their royal master and to his loyal subjects. I will treat with none of these. Such is my answer.'

In an attempt to break this spirited defiance, Wardour was bombarded for five days. Lady Blanche marshalled her 25 men against 1300 Parliamentarians. Her daughter-in-law Cecily, along with the maidservants, reloaded the weapons after each round of fire, while Lady Blanche rallied her forces each morning after Mass with an exhortation to return every shot with a volley.

The siege had, however, caught Wardour quite unprepared. There were no provisions of food, water or ammunition laid in and on May 8, with sixty of the attacking force dead, Lady Blanche was forced to surrender.

Fearful lest her son, by now the third Lord Arundell, should try to recapture Wardour, the Parliamentarians left Edmund Ludlow to defend the newly-won prize. And for almost a year, Lord Arundell was encamped in the shadow of his ancestral home, struggling to muster enough men to attempt to storm the castle. Having failed in that task, he resorted to desperate measures, effectively placing a bomb under Wardour to compel Ludlow to surrender, but in the process reducing the castle to the ruin which can still be seen today.

The Arundells were left homeless and had to make do with some of the old outbuildings which had survived the blast. Unbowed, they continued among the ruins to practise their religion in defiance of the law as they had done since Elizabethan times.

Sir Thomas Arundell in particular had earned the queen's disapproval when, in recognition of his heroism in repelling the Ottoman Turks from Hungary in 1595, he was created a Count of the Holy Roman Empire and received by the Pope. Elizabeth was enraged at what she saw as Arundell's disloyalty in accepting a foreign title and had him imprisoned. 'As chaste wives should have no glances but for their own spouses,' she is reported to have remarked, 'so should faithful subjects keep their eyes at home and not gaze on foreign crowns.'

He survived the queen's disapproval. The third Lord Arundell was made of no less stern stuff. He was imprisoned briefly in the Tower of London in 1678 after Titus Oates had implicated him in an imaginary plot to replace Charles II as king with a Catholic. Oates, an adventurer who had infiltrated the seminaries at Valladolid in Spain and Saint Omer in France, claimed to have uncovered a plan to murder Charles. His unfounded accusations led to the execution of many innocent men.

Arundell later was named Keeper of the Privy Seal by James II when he succeeded his brother Charles in 1685. James's avowed intent of restoring legal rights to Catholics jeopardized his throne, however, and in the 'Glorious Revolution' of 1688 he was replaced by the Protestants William and Mary. Arundell's grandson Thomas was killed fighting in James's rear-guard action in Ireland at the Battle of the Boyne in 1690.

For the next century the Lords Arundell lived a quiet life, prohibited by the Test Act from holding public office and subject to the double land tax imposed on them by William's Parliament. Like many Catholic families of the time, they managed to survive financially only by dint of a series of advantageous marriages.

They continued too to hold Catholic Masses in the ruins of Wardour with the help of a series of Jesuits who lived there at first covertly and later more openly, as penal restrictions were relaxed and the Stuart threat faded into history. Wardour became known as one of the largest Catholic Mass centres outside London and when, in 1770, Henry Arundell, the eighth baron, felt wealthy enough to build a new home next to what was left of the old castle, the chapel took up one whole wing.

The Jesuit historian Philip Caraman has written that Wardour 'is proof that Catholics in the eighteenth century were left free to build as they wished'. Henry Arundell wanted a grand house and chose for the task James Paine, the leading English disciple of the Italian architect Andrea Palladio.

When it came to the chapel, Paine's austere and decidedly un-church-like exterior was complimented by a lavish interior designed by Giacomo Quarenghi and later augmented by Sir John Soane. Quarenghi, subsequently employed by Catherine the Great on the Peterhof Palace, the State Bank and the Hermitage Theatre in her imperial capital, Saint Petersburg, was assisted in his task by an English Jesuit, Father John Thorpe, then resident in Rome. It was Thorpe who commissioned the altar built in the Roman workshop of Giacomo Quirenza, and Thorpe too who obtained for Wardour the altarpiece which once stood in the private chapel of the Jesuit Superior General.

The opening ceremony on All Saints Day 1776 for what was always intended as a parish church was one of the biggest public celebrations staged by English Catholics since pre-Reformation days. But four years later the passage of the first Catholic Relief Act triggered the Gordon Riots and the church was threatened by a mob crying 'No Popery'. Lord Arundell had to arrange for a keeper of the peace to be in attendance at all services there.

In 1790, Sir John Soane – best remembered today for the Bank of

England building – enlarged the sanctuary of the church and added some exterior ornament. Thorpe again was consulted and sent his approval, adding that Wardour could now be considered a basilica. Records indicate that it was then serving no less than 540 Catholics.

John Francis Arundell, the sixteenth baron, was just 31 when he succeeded his father in 1939. Wounded and captured by the Germans in France the following year, his repeated attempts to escape meant that he was consigned to Colditz where his health broke down. He died in Chester in a military hospital in 1944 without ever seeing Wardour again.

Following his death the Arundell property was disposed of, first to the Jesuits and later to Cranborne Chase School for Girls. When this closed, Wardour was sold for division into luxury flats. The church continues to be used for worship by the local parish each Sunday at 10.30 and is held in trust. A recent appeal, supported by various well-known artists who contributed their impressions of the church, has allowed vital works to be carried out on the roof of this historic and still well-attended Catholic centre of worship.

BOSCOBEL HOUSE

SHROPSHIRE

While Boscobel, her balm, by Night,
Lenient and Loyal, dar'd to shed,
And momentarily guarded the Monarch's bed
Asylum for a King (Anon 1800)

EVERY schoolchild remembers the story of Charles II hiding in an oak tree. After his defeat at Worcester in 1651, he fled the battlefield with Cromwell's men hard on his heels. He evaded them by sheltering in a tree in the grounds of Boscobel, before finding a more comfortable billet in the house itself. The woods around Boscobel did not only protect the king, though, they kept this historic house from prying eyes and enabled it to be used as a refuge for Catholic priests.

Boscobel was built around 1630 by a recusant Catholic, John Giffard. Thomas Blount's account of Charles's escape, written in 1660, tells us that Giffard named his new home Boscobel 'from the Italian *bosco bello*, because it is seated in the midst of a fair woods'. He describes the house as 'a very obscure habitation', a reference that could be taken geographically or archi-tecturally. Tall and elaborately framed, Boscobel is essentially modest in proportion, a two-storey L-shaped hunting lodge whose timbered exterior disappeared behind stucco rendering in the eighteenth century.

Designed to provide Giffard and his guests with a bed after a day's hunting, this remote house offered a perfect place for concealing missionary priests. While several of the original hiding places in the house have subse-quently disappeared during renovations, two still exist, one in the Squire's Bedroom and the other in the attic.

By the time of Charles's unannounced visit in September 1651, with his hopes of installing himself as king in succession to his executed father now in tatters, John Giffard had died. Boscobel had passed to his daughter Frances and her husband John Cotton. They lived elsewhere and left it in the hands of caretakers, William and Joan Penderel.

It was, however, well-known to at least three of Charles's party as they made their escape from Worcester. One was the Earl of Derby, who had rested at Boscobel after the Battle of Wigan a few weeks earlier. The second was John Giffard's kinsman, Charles Giffard, who agreed to act as the king's guide once Boscobel had been suggested. And the third was Giffard's servant, Francis Yates, who stood by his master and later paid for his loyalty with his life.

Anxious to cover their tracks, the royal party was taken by Giffard first to White Ladies' Priory, another Cotton house about half a mile beyond Boscobel. Today only the ruins of this nunnery's medieval church remain.

At the Priory, the king disguised himself, as he later recalled, in 'a pair of ordinary grey-cloth breeches, a leather doublet and a green jerkin'. Giffard had sent for Penderel and his brother to guide the king to Boscobel. 'He was a Roman Catholic,' the king told Samuel Pepys in 1680, 'and I chose to trust them because I knew they had hiding holes for priests that I thought I might make use of in case of need.'

Charles obviously had a sixth sense for no sooner had they left the Priory than they spotted a detachment of Cromwell's troops and were forced to take refuge in Spring Coppice in pouring rain for the rest of the day. To fill the empty hours Charles was taught to walk and talk like a yokel.

Come nightfall and the king made his way first to a house in Madeley, also owned by Catholics and with a priest-hole. But this had been discovered and the monarch was forced to sleep in the barn. From there the party headed for Boscobel.

They arrived at three in the morning and Penderel went on ahead to check that the coast was clear. He discovered that another refugee from Worcester had already sought shelter at Boscobel. Major William Careless, like the Giffards a recusant Catholic, settled down with the king for bread and cheese and 'a Posset of thin milk and smal beer'. Charles there learnt that his diplomatic envoy, Lord Wilmot, was being cared for by another Catholic family in the vicinity.

At daybreak, the fugitives once more sheltered in the woods fearing that Boscobel might be searched. Charles hid in the branches of an oak tree 'that had been lopt some three or four years before and being grown out again, very bushy and thick, could not be seen through'. Some 150 yards southwest of Boscobel House today stands a tree known as 'the Royal Oak', though it is believed to be the offspring of an acorn from the original tree which was hacked down by souvenir hunters in the eighteenth century.

That evening the king once again slept under Boscobel's roof, hidden in the priest-hole in the attic, just four foot by four foot by three foot four and known now as 'the Cheese Room'. Legend has it that on one occasion the pursuivants brought bloodhounds to Boscobel to sniff out priests, but were put off the scent once they reached the attic by cheese stored as a decoy in the hide.

The next day, after feasting on mutton chops, the king, accompanied by five Penderel brothers, set off on a borrowed mill-horse for the house of Mr Whitegreave, a Catholic, at Moseley. The scene is incised in black marble over the parlour fireplace in Boscobel. At Moseley Old Hall he was greeted by his host and the resident Catholic priest, Father John Huddlestone. After two days Charles set off for Bristol and thence to exile in France. On his deathbed in 1685 he met Fr Huddlestone again and was, many believe, received into the Catholic Church.

It is ironic that Charles, later a persecutor of Catholics as his father and grandfather before him, should not only have been rescued by Catholics and sheltered alongside a missionary priest but that he was concealed in a hide designed to protect Catholic clergymen from agents of the Crown. Despite being regarded as traitors since the time of Elizabeth, Catholics remained ardent Royalists.

Fortunately, the Penderels survived the aftermath of the king's flight. Boscobel and White Ladies were searched and the brothers questioned. Only Francis Yates, their brother-in-law, fell foul of the authorities and was executed. After the Restoration, Charles granted the Penderels a pension in perpetuity and it is paid to this day.

They continued to live at Boscobel throughout the eighteenth century, using the attic as a chapel and playing host to various Jesuit missions. The ownership passed through marriage from the Cottons to the Fitzherberts of Norbury – whose story we tell elsewhere.

Boscobel's hide was one of the first to go on display. In 1686 Robert Plot refers to it in his *Natural History of Staffordshire* (the house straddles the border with Shropshire).

The Earl of Bradford bought the house in 1918 and placed it in the care of the Ministry of Works in 1954. Since 1984, it has been in the hands of English Heritage who have restored and refurbished it. The first floor of the North Range contains an award-winning exhibition which tells the story of the king's escape, surely one of the most dramatic and romantic stories in English history.

THE EIGHTEENTH CENTURY
OUT OF THE SHADOWS

WARDLEY HALL

GREATER MANCHESTER

*The Holy Virgin's Offspring and Master of the House adorned with
the martyr's head, after an exile of three hundred years, when the
sacrifice (Mass) was offered on His birthday (Christmas Day) 1930,
Thomas – Bishop – with joy was able to make return unto his own*
Plaque in Wardley to mark the return of the Blessed Sacrament

W ARDLEY Hall, a brown-and-white half-timbered manor house,
built during the reign of the ultra-Protestant Edward VI and today
the residence of the Catholic Bishops of Salford, has been better known for
the past 200 years as 'the House of the Skull'. Protected by a wooded estate in
Worsley, six miles northwest of the centre of Manchester, the hall contains a
human skull, kept for generations in a niche at the side of the main staircase.
It has been the subject both of Catholic veneration and bizarre legend.

The mystery that surrounds the skull's origins is complicated by the
history of Wardley itself. The hall has passed through many families since it
was built by Thurston Tyldesley 500 years ago on the site of an earlier
medieval house.

A minor incident during the Jacobite revolt of 1745 first brought the skull to light. The rebel army under Bonnie Prince Charlie was encamped near to Wardley Hall in a spot now known as 'Rebel Field'. A detachment arrived at the hall, then occupied by Matthew Moreton, a tenant farmer, to demand carts and horses.

Though Wardley then enjoyed the protection of a moat – which still exists to the south and west of the house – it did not deter the Jacobites from forcing Moreton to do their bidding. As a result he was ruined financially. In desperation, he turned part of the hall over to hand looms in an attempt to make good his losses. When the builders were creating a workroom out of what had once been a secret chapel they came upon a chest buried in the walls. It contained a skull.

Despite its auburn hair and set of teeth, it was mistaken by a housemaid for an animal's skull and thrown into the moat. That night, though, there was a terrible storm and Moreton became convinced that it had been caused by the skull. He had the moat drained the next day so that he could find the skull and restore it to its original resting place in the hall.

From this incident grew a tradition that if the skull was moved or treated disrespectfully 'such commotions arose about the house that no one dared live in it'. Fletcher Moss in his *Pilgrimages to Old Homes* continues: 'Windows were blown in, cattle pined in the stall and things were bewitched...There is plenty of testimony to the ill-luck that has happened when the skull has been disturbed; and this has not come from the superstitious only, but from shrewd observant men of business whose word is as good as their bond.'

The skull was for a long time said to belong to Roger Downes whose family lived at Wardley during the middle decades of the seventeenth century. The son of devout Catholics, Roger grew up to be one of the most

Ince Blundell Hall: the southern aspect.

Ingatestone Hall: the view from the gatehouse.

Stonyhurst: the chapel and the monks' burial ground.

abandoned and vicious courtiers of Charles II. During one drunken binge, he is supposed to have sworn that he would kill the next man he met. As he staggered through the streets, he bumped into a poor tailor and ran him through with his sword.

His position at court saved him from trial but he got his just desserts shortly afterwards when he was decapitated in a brawl in Epsom Wells. The story went that someone sent his head to his sister at Wardley and that, although it was at various times removed from the hall, it would invariably return.

However, when this theory was tested in the eighteenth century and the Downes's family vault in Wigan opened, Roger's skeleton was found in one piece. Since then the general consensus has favoured the skull belonging to Father Ambrose Barlow, a Jesuit priest who was hung, drawn and quartered in Lancaster on September 7, 1641.

Born in Manchester in 1585 Ambrose Barlow trained as a priest on the Continent and after his ordination returned secretly – and in defiance of the law of the land – to Lancashire to minister to the persecuted Catholic families. A relative of the Downes family, he was welcomed and given shelter at Wardley.

Ambrose knew the risks of his mission. He once said of martyrdom: 'I have bidden as fair for it as another.' He was arrested while saying Mass on Easter Sunday in 1641 and after his gruesome death that autumn, his head was put on a spike and displayed to the populace of Manchester.

It seems quite possible that Francis Downes of Wardley Hall, Ambrose's kinsman, rescued the head and kept it in his secret chapel. Francis was by then an old man and in 1648 was succeeded by his brother Roger, likewise an unreformed Catholic. Roger died shortly afterwards. His children, the aforementioned sword-happy Roger and his sister Penelope, were – like

Richard Hoghton and many others before them – raised as Protestants in accordance with the laws of the day.

With Roger's death at Epsom, Wardley passed out of the Downes family and its grisly relic was forgotten until the fateful day, almost a century later, when the skull tumbled out of the rubble. Forensic tests carried out on the skull at Saint Bartholomew's College in London in 1960 indicate that it belonged to a man of Ambrose's age and stature, and that it had been violently severed from the body after death and stuck on something like a spike or a lance. Ambrose was also reputed to have had auburn hair. Though no final proof has ever been forthcoming, for many Catholics the skull is now a religious relic.

In 1930, the Catholic diocese of Salford, covering the Greater Manchester region, bought a part of the Wardley estate for use as a cemetery. At the same time the then owner, Captain Thomas Nutall, made a gift of the hall itself and its grounds to the diocese.

TRAQUAIR HOUSE

PEEBLESSHIRE

The wild rose twines on the gateway there,
The green weed grows and the bramble clings,
Barring the road to thy hearth, Traquair,
With loyal hands of the earth's green things;
The wind through the rusted iron sings,
The sun on the self sown tangle burns,
But never a hoof on the roadway rings -
The gate is shut till the King returns.
Till the King Returns by W. H. Ogilvie

MANY legends have been woven around Traquair. Its origins are a mystery though it is reputed to be the oldest inhabited house in Scotland. Its royal pedigree is, however, impeccable.

Traquair's grey walls have sheltered kings and queens of Scotland since Alexander I in 1107. The King's Room in the twelfth-century tower contains the state bed where Mary Queen of Scots slept in 1566. At its foot is the cot she used for her baby son, the future King James VI of Scotland, James I of England. But it is for the story of the Bear Gates and a king who never was that Traquair is best remembered.

Popular tradition has it that Bonnie Prince Charlie, grandson of James II, the last Catholic king of England, visited Traquair in the Scottish Borders in 1745 during his abortive attempt to claim the throne. The Stuart pretender exhorted his kinsman the fifth Earl of Traquair, Charles Stuart, to come out on his side with more vigour. The earl remained calm, the story goes, threw the keys to Traquair into the River Tweed and then pointed to the Bear Gates. He promised that they would not be reopened until the Stuarts were restored to their kingdom. They have remained closed to this day.

The story may be true. The fifth earl was indeed an ardent Jacobite. He spent two years in the Tower of London after the '45 and was obliged to pay for his own rooms and food, an imposition that caused him considerable financial hardship. The gates themselves, the 'Steekit Yetts' with simple railings and carved stone bears, were erected in 1737, and so were *in situ* at the time of the 1745 rising.

Yet dispute has surrounded their place in history. Certainly they were never used after 1745 when a ford across the Tweed became an alternative route, bypassing the tree-lined avenue that leads to them.

There is, though, no hard evidence that Bonnie Prince Charlie came to Traquair. It may have been that the gates were closed to commemorate the failed 1745 rising.

Alternatively, Sir Walter Scott, the romantic novelist who had a family link with Traquair, held that the gates had been closed in protest at laws enacted fining Catholics who kept carriage horses.

Another theory has it that the gates were closed by the seventh Earl in 1796 after the funeral of his young wife. He is reported to have said that they would not be reopened until they could receive another Countess of Traquair, an event that never happened. The fact that the last Countess died while living with the rest of her family in Spain would seem to cast doubt on this version.

The eighth Earl did not marry but lived at Traquair with his sister Lady Louisa Stuart until his death in 1860. To a visitor who went to Traquair in this period, the house, like the Stuart dynasty, 'seemed dying out, everything subdued to desolation. The old race, the old religion, the gaunt old house with its small, deep, comfortless windows, the decaying trees, the stillness about the doors, the grass overrunning everything'. When Lady Louisa died in 1875 in her nineties, the house passed to a cousin, Henry Constable Maxwell who added Stuart to his surname as a consequence. Lady Louisa is reported to have travelled around her relatives in search of a suitable heir, peering into their faces to detect an appealing sign.

Traquair House had been home to the Stuarts since 1513 when James Stuart fell with the 'Flowers of the Forest' at Flodden. The family did not become Catholic until the 1650s, but their choice of religion was a turning point in their long-term fortunes and it went hand-in-hand with their later Jacobitism.

The second Earl of Traquair married into Catholicism. Indeed, both his brides were Catholic. His first marriage earned him fines and imprisonment and his second, to Lady Anne Seton in 1654, established a Catholic tradition at Traquair which continues to this day. On his deathbed, the second earl wrote to his children directing them to the 'true religion'. The letter is preserved at the house.

During the seventeenth-century persecutions, the family heard Mass in secret. A priest's room with a hidden staircase can be viewed by the public. The shelved cupboard by the north window has a false back. This leads down a staircase to the ground floor and out through a side exit thus affording a quick escape route for any priest sheltering in Traquair.

When the 'Glorious Revolution' of 1688 swept away James II and the Stuart dynasty, Traquair saw violence for the first time. A document kept in the house's chapel – built after emancipation – lists the religious artefacts destroyed when an anti-popish mob from Peebles raided the house. The plate, books and devotional objects were burnt at the Cross in Peebles. Charles, the fourth earl, was then 29 and it was under him and his wife, Lady Mary Maxwell, that the house became a centre of Jacobitism in the Borders.

Their initials can be seen on the intricately worked front door knocker. It was made in 1705 and thus disproves another pet theory of Sir Walter Scott. He claimed that the knocker was used by the Royalist General Montrose at the time of the Civil War. Hotly pursued by an army of Covenanters who had decimated his small force of Cavaliers at the Battle of Philiphaugh, he turned up at Traquair one autumn day in 1645 and hammered on the door, begging for sanctuary.

John Stuart, the first Earl of Traquair and Lord High Treasurer and High Commissioner under Charles I, was believed to be inside but Montrose's pleas were ignored and the door was kept bolted. The Covenanters massacred 300 wounded men, prisoners, women, children and servants fleeing from the battlefield. Montrose was fortunate to escape with his life.

The Earl's actions may have saved Traquair from destruction but they took a heavy toll on his conscience and reputation. The man whose portrait hangs in the Dining Room ended his days a beggar while his honour has been disputed by his countrymen ever after.

However, his Catholic descendants were possessed of the courage he appeared to lack and their loyalty to the Stuart cause is recalled in Traquair's collection of Jacobite glass, which is on display in the Museum Room with a rosary and crucifix that belonged to Mary Queen of Scots.

The house today is owned – and supported – by Flora Maxwell Stuart.

Ince Blundell Hall

MERSEYSIDE

Catholicity survived in Lancashire not only because of the staunch-
ness proper to its people, the tenacity with which they cling to old
traditions, but because the Faith itself is the very marrow of their
being

Dom F. O. Blundell 'Old Catholic Lancashire'

STANDING behind its high red-brick wall as an island of space
and order amid the clutter of the suburban sprawl of Liverpool,
Ince Blundell Hall and its 50-acre park were for generations the home
of one of Lancashire's leading recusant families, the Blundells. Here
behind an imposing three-storey brick and stone façade, they maintained until the latter half of the twentieth century an aristocratic and
devout life.

Like many Lancastrians from all levels of society, the Blundells who had
inhabited the manor of Ince since the thirteenth century, refused to
compromise in their allegiance to the Pope at the time of Henry VIII's break
with Rome. When Elizabeth's spies and pursuivants hounded them in their

twelfth-century manor house – the shell of which survives to this day in the park – the Blundells secretly built a small chapel deep in the woods, where, in the shadow of its cross-shaped windows, they continued the practice of centuries.

For the main part the family worked away quietly, profitably but unspectacularly in the professions. However, with the gradual relaxation of the penal measures against Catholics, Robert Blundell felt confident enough in 1720 to begin the construction of a new home 100 yards away from his manor house.

Ince Blundell Hall is designed along Georgian lines and in imitation of the original Buckingham House in London. Though Robert may have been comfortable with parading his wealth by building such a handsome new home, he still saw the need to maintain a low profile when it came to religion. Sensitive to any suggestion of evangelizing, he did not feel able openly to include a chapel in the grand design. Instead, at the end of what was the servants' block, behind the main house, you can still climb the staircase that once led to a small oratory hidden away, with no outward show, under the gables.

The steps today lead to an organ loft, part of the grand nineteenth-century chapel, designed by J. J. Scoles, which replaced the earlier place of worship once all remaining fears and prejudices had been overcome. In the eighteenth century, the Blundells played host to the Jesuits who used the hall as one of the centres of their Lancastrian mission.

In the last quarter of the eighteenth century, Henry Blundell added Ince Blundell's Pantheon, its most intriguing and ostentatious architectural feature. Its scale was another indication of the growing confidence of the English Catholic gentry who were now given legal rights by the Relief Acts of 1778 and 1791 to buy and inherit land. The day of full equality was still fifty years away but Henry Blundell saw no need to temper his taste for display.

The Pantheon was designed to house his extensive collection of antiquities which he built up in rivalry with his Catholic neighbour, Charles Towneley of Towneley Hall. While Blundell may have commissioned the grander showcase, Towneley amassed the more interesting collection and his treasures are now in the British Museum. Blundell's legacy was given to the city of Liverpool by his descendants in 1959.

In 1837 Henry's heir Charles Robert died and the male Blundell line came to an end. The estate could not be inherited by a woman so it passed to a distant cousin Thomas Weld, a junior member of the recusant clan of Lulworth Castle in Dorset. The one condition for the inheritance was that the heir changed his surname to Weld-Blundell.

Charles Blundell's two sisters – both married into long-standing Catholic families, one to a Stonor and the other a Tempest of Broughton Hall – resolved to contest the will, so passionately did they feel about their home. They launched what became a celebrated legal battle and were finally defeated in the House of Lords. (One sister had died by the time of the court case but her nephew continued the fight.)

The ruling turned out to be a godsend for Ince Blundell for Thomas Weld-Blundell oversaw extensive renovations to the house. He employed the celebrated interior designer Crace to adorn several of the main rooms with pretty Raphaelesque motifs and fashioned a perfectly proportioned gallery which is today used as a chapel for private prayer.

Thomas and his wife Teresa were both deeply devout and are recalled by stained-glass windows of their patron saints in the main chapel. Their twelve children and numerous grandchildren continued to live at Ince Blundell while the hall was a landmark for the local Catholic community at a time when Liverpool was welcoming wave after wave of Irish immigration. The main chapel acted as a parish church and is today owned by the Archdiocese of Liverpool.

The last two Weld-Blundell male heirs died during and shortly after the First World World. For forty years the house entered something of a twilight zone, home to their two grieving sisters for their lifetime but fated to be sold on their deaths. Proud of the family tradition both women insisted – unusually for the time – that they kept their maiden name when they married. The two were determined that the house should be used for religious purposes and persuaded the heirs, their Weld cousins from Lulworth, to favour some kind of apostolic work for the future of Ince Blundell.

In 1958 when the second Weld-Blundell sister died, John Carmel Heenan, the then Archbishop of Liverpool and later Cardinal Archbishop of Westminster, managed to persuade the Augustinian Nursing Sisters, a French order, to buy the property despite interest from the Littlewoods founder, John Moores. The sisters continue to run it as a home for retired priests and lay people and have been sensitive when carrying out essential alterations to maintain the character of what was for many years one of the grandest Catholic houses in Lancashire.

Ingatestone Hall

ESSEX

Sans Dieu Rien
(Nothing Without God)
Petre family motto

Nestling long and low-beamed in the Essex countryside, tucked behind formal hedges and approached by a meandering lane, Ingatestone Hall managed to hide itself away from the worst excesses of the Catholic persecution. This Tudor mansion has its priest-holes and its martyrs, but the heroism of Ingatestone and of its owners, the Petre family, is of the quiet and unsung variety, working round obstacles placed in the path of recusants to keep hearth and home together.

In the eighteenth century the family re-emerged from obscurity to take a leading role in the rehabilitation of Catholics in royal and national esteem. The ninth Lord Petre chaired the Committee of Catholic Laymen which negotiated the Catholic Relief Act of June 1778. This legislation removed the ban on Catholics buying and inheriting land and abolished the statutory life sentence for anyone caught functioning as a Catholic priest or running a Catholic school.

In what was taken as a mark of royal approval for this measure, and as a sign of a new social acceptability of Catholics, George III and Queen Charlotte stayed with the Petres in October 1778. 'I shall always hold it as the most flattering circumstance of my life', Lord Petre wrote later of the visit, 'that His Majesty gave me an opportunity of showing him in the ordinary course of life that respect, loyalty and affection which the laws of my country prevent me from doing on more important occurrences.'

Lord Petre played host to the king at Thorndon Hall, the Palladian mansion in Essex that was for 300 years the principal family seat. But just as important in the story of the Petres' recusancy is their original – and, after a devastating fire at Thorndon in 1876, current – home at Ingatestone.

The founder of the dynasty, William Petre, had assisted Thomas Cromwell in the Dissolution of the Monasteries in 1535. Despite this, and his subsequent appointment as Secretary of State by Henry VIII, he held firm to his Catholicism. Like Sir Walter Stonor and Sir Antony Fitzherbert of Norbury, he managed to balance public life with private conscience.

While drawing up a list of the monasteries of southern England, William was particularly taken by the manor of Ingatestone, part of the patrimony of Barking Abbey. In 1539 he purchased the property, paying the king by instalments. He thereby – albeit technically – avoided benefiting financially from Henry's brutal religious policy.

William demolished the existing manor house at Ingatestone and erected in its place a red-brick mansion around a central courtyard. The outer shell is substantially unchanged today save for the demolition of the West Wing in the middle of the eighteenth century.

With William's death in 1571, the house passed to his widow while his son and heir moved to Thorndon. Seemingly emboldened by widowhood – rather like Eleanor Brookesby and Cecily Stonor – Lady Mary Petre allowed Ingatestone to be used as an illegal base for the missionary priests from the Continent. Chief among her guests was the Jesuit John Payne, subsequently hanged, drawn and quartered at Chelmsford in 1582.

Though the house boasts two priest-holes, one behind panelling in the study and the other tucked away adjacent to a staircase, it is thought these were used only to store vestments and church plate in case of a raid by Elizabeth's priest-hunters. Ingatestone also possesses a collection of recusant chalices – so called because they were made to a small scale so as to be portable – and a crucifix reputed to have been held by Mary Queen of Scots at her execution. Her chaplain was a cousin of the Petres.

In the years after Elizabeth I's death, the Petres continued to live quietly at Thorndon with junior branches of the family at Ingatestone. They survived fines and sequestrations at the hands of Oliver Cromwell and the imprisonment of the fourth Baron Petre for his alleged involvement in the so-called Popish Plot of 1678.

The nearest the Petres got to treason was through their involvement with the ill-fated Earl of Derwenter. The father-in-law of the Lord Petre of the day, he took part in the Jacobite Rebellion of 1715, an attempt to install on the throne James The Old Pretender, son of James II. It failed and Derwenter's death mask and the clothes he wore at his execution are kept at Ingatestone.

Excluded from the expensive business of politics and enriched by a series of judicious marriages, the Petres were at the time of George III's visit one of the richest families in the country. Robert Petre, the ninth Baron, married the heiress Anne Howard, daughter of the Duke of Norfolk. Her fortune allowed him to rebuild Thorndon with a Corinthian portico in the grand style of the period. It could have been the home of any of the great Whig magnates – save for its richly ornamented Catholic chapel.

The twelfth Baron Petre was an enthusiastic builder of churches around Essex and he twice, in the middle years of the nineteenth century, extended the chapel at Ingatestone which continued to serve as a parish church for the locality until 1932.

His son and heir was ordained a priest and taught at the Benedictine school of Downside in Somerset where a library, a cloister and, unusually for the nineteenth century, a swimming pool recall his individual generosity and the more general role of the Petre family in financing the re-establishment of Catholicism in bricks and mortar around England.

Ingatestone today is now home to the Honourable Dominic Petre, heir to the title. His parents, the current Lord and Lady Petre, live with their other children at nearby Writtle Park.

STONYHURST

LANCASHIRE

Old Alma Mater, here's to thee!
Stonyhurst! Old Stonyhurst!
Long life and all prosperity!
Stonyhurst! Old Stonyhurst!
While generations come and go,
While boyhood doth to manhood grow,
Be aye the same we used to know,
Stonyhurst, Old Stonyhurst!
School Song - late nineteenth century

ONE of the harshest of the penal measures against English Catholics was the denial of their right to educate their children as they saw fit. Recusant Catholics were faced with the choice of either sending their offspring to establishments whose central purpose was to inculcate Protestantism into the young or smuggling them out of the country – in defiance of the law and at the risk of hefty fines – for a Catholic schooling on the Continent.

For those who chose the later course, the most popular destination was the Jesuit college at Saint Omer in northern France, opened by Father Robert Persons with money from the King of Spain in 1593. There generation after generation of young English Catholic males received a classical education.

The curriculum was not only scholarly, however. When they went back to their ancestral homes the old boys of Saint Omer were acutely aware of the continuing history of the persecution and their special role in keeping the flickering flame of faith alight. Moreover they were ready, should the need arise, to shelter their former mentors during their cloak and dagger missions to the faithful in England.

In 1762, political upheavals on the Continent and the suppression of the Jesuits by Pope Clement XIV forced the school to move to Bruges and later to Liège. The removal of the ban on Catholic schools in the two Relief Acts of 1778 and 1791 had encouraged thoughts of returning home. Circumstances made a decision urgent. When a generous donor presented himself in the shape of Thomas Weld, one of the richest Catholics in the country, the die was cast.

Weld, an old boy from Bruges days, had inherited from his Shireburn relatives the manor house of Stonyhurst outside Blackburn in Lancashire. It had a noble history of defending the old religion and included under its roof several priest-holes. But Weld was happily ensconced at Lulworth Castle in Dorset and had no particular use for Stonyhurst. He was therefore happy to grant the school a lease.

When the Jesuits arrived the house had been empty for almost 40 years since the death of the Dowager Duchess of Norfolk, the last of the Shireburns. As the advance party made their way up the formal avenue, laid out by Nicholas Shireburn in 1696, they must have remarked on the curious façade of their new home. The Shireburns had planned to complete the grand quadrangle of their original Elizabethan manor house. But the fines they had incurred killed off such dreams and Stonyhurst was left half-finished, the new North Wing leading on to a triumphant gatehouse, with cupolas topped by eagles, but unbalanced by anything on the other side.

Grace Dieu Manor: the southern aspect.

Mount Stuart: the view from the woodland garden.

Tichborne House.

Right: The chapel on the west side.

Though Turner gave the original Stonyhurst a romantic and pastoral air in his watercolour of 1799 – an engraving of which hangs today in the 'Do' Room, a gallery beneath the Old Refectory – Oliver Cromwell was perhaps nearer the mark when he described it as the finest half-house he had ever seen. Cromwell had imposed himself and his men on the Royalist Shireburns in 1648 on his way to the Battle of Preston. A long oak table where he is reputed to have slept is on display today.

For the Jesuits, though, Stonyhurst was ideal. Its rural location, under the shadow of Pendle Hill, meant that they could go about their work out of sight and out of mind of the southern Lancashire mill-towns with their Puritanism and anti-Catholicism.

In keeping with the mood of the English Catholicism in the early decades of the nineteenth century, the Jesuits avoided any confrontation by keeping a low profile and added small, solid if unspectacular buildings to the original Shireburn mansion, giving the whole site the feel of a village.

In the summer of 1810, an elderly Thomas Weld came to see what had been made of his gift. In high spirits at dinner that night, he responded to cheers from the boys with a chorus of 'I am Mad Tom, Behold Me' and promptly keeled over and died. His anniversary is still marked each year at the school.

Weld had made over the Stonyhurst estate to the Jesuits and with the changing mood in the country after the passage of the 1829 Emancipation Act, they felt able to add a little ornament to their new headquarters. The Church of Saint Peter, in Perpendicular Gothic style and modelled on King's College Chapel in Cambridge, was built between 1832 and 1835 by J. J. Scoles, also responsible for the chapel at Ince Blundell.

Two years later came the Observatory building and in 1857 the Ambulacrum, one of the first indoor sports halls in the country and a practical if visionary solution to the problem of exercising young boys when it was raining outside. In 1857 the front quadrangle was finally completed.

In spite of all this building, however, there was still a residual fear among the Jesuits of putting on too great a show. The priest poet Gerard Manley Hopkins, while studying philosophy at St Mary's Hall, the seminary attached to Stonyhurst, recalled his induction to the noviciate which until 1855 was based at Hodder Place, one mile from the college. 'In a tiny chapel upstairs, lit by a skylight...Father Fitzsimon sat near a small table on which stood a crucifix, and we entered singly one after another, as though going to confession, and kneeling down took our vows in secret...The Master of Novices merely answered Amen and took the written formula of the vow and the young religious withdrew.'

It may have been this continuing air of secrecy, not to mention the heavy mists that swirl over the property from nearby hills, that inspired one of its old boys, the mystery writer Sir Arthur Conan Doyle. It has been claimed that he based Baskerville Hall, echoing to the sound of the infamous hound, on Stonyhurst.

All caution was thrown to the wind in 1888 though when the Jesuits commissioned the building of the ostentatious south wing to a design by Dunn and Hansom in a splendidly over-the-top Victorian pastiche of Renaissance-style architecture. It is believed to be the largest single scholastic façade in England and was inspired, some have speculated, less by shortage of space than by a perceived need to trumpet Stonyhurst's status.

Indeed, the twentieth century has seen the school take its place alongside the great public schools of England. In 1985, Stonyhurst appointed its first lay head, though the Jesuits remain actively involved. When, in 1990, Her Majesty The Queen paid a visit, it seemed like a sign that the wounds of the past had finally been healed.

As Giles Mercer, the present head, writes in a recent history of the school: 'The College, though thoroughly English, began in detachment from the mainstream of national life, almost as a counterforce to it, and then gradually over the centuries found itself able to open out to a wider society. The history of Stonyhurst is in this respect a microcosm of the post-Reformation history of the Catholic Church in England and Wales.'

THE NINETEENTH CENTURY

EMANCIPATION AND THE RECONVERSION OF ENGLAND?

Grace Dieu Manor

LEICESTERSHIRE

The Catholic Church, she never knew –
Till Mr Pugin taught her,
That orthodoxy had to do
At all with bricks and mortar
Song on Pugin's 'Contrasts'

Tucked away behind a screen of trees on the edge of Charnwood Forest, Grace Dieu Manor has always echoed to the laughter of children. Today run by the Rosminian order as a Catholic prep school, William Railton's Tudor Gothic manor house was the first marital home of the noted nineteenth-century convert Ambrose Lisle March Phillipps, his wife and their sixteen children.

Ambrose was born into the bosom of the English Establishment, son of a Member of Parliament, scion of an old Leicestershire land-owning family. In 1825, however, at the tender age of sixteen, he outraged his father and broke every convention of his class by becoming a Roman Catholic. It was a brave act. Catholics were not granted full civil rights until 1829 and

Ambrose knew no other lay Catholics at the time of his conversion. Indeed he was one of the few Catholic undergraduates at Cambridge University.

The determined teenager matured into a tireless worker for the revival of the 'old religion' in England. He was one of a trio of outstanding lay leaders in the vanguard of English Catholicism in the years after emancipation, the others being John Talbot, the sixteenth Earl of Shrewsbury, and the architect Augustus Welby Pugin. They shared a passion for medieval Catholicism and saw a revival of Gothic art, architecture and liturgy as the route to recapturing the past. As part of that drive, Grace Dieu became a centre for Catholic liturgy and proselytizing.

It was Ambrose who first persuaded the Rosminian order to send a mission to England. They arrived in 1835, the year Grace Dieu was completed, though their first base was at the theological college at Prior Park in Somerset. Their leader was the remarkable Italian, Aloysius Gentili, who did not immediately warm to Protestant England. 'In this country', he wrote to a friend, 'though it has fallen so low, our religion has a great harvest, but is without labourers...all is melancholy, a heavy atmosphere hangs over a monotonous countryside, the poverty is frightening.'

Gentili was less than diplomatic in introducing a new regime of austerity and the local bishop was persuaded to sack him. He then turned to his patron, Ambrose, and was welcomed to Grace Dieu as chaplain. The transfer was accompanied, however, by a few words of advice to Gentili from Ambrose. In order to foster better relations with the English, it was suggested, the Italian Rosminian might wash more often and shave occasionally. Gentili took such concerns for vanity but Ambrose insisted that a scruffy priest would not make the impact they both so desired.

Rosminian missions were eventually set up in Shepshed and then Loughborough. By that stage Ambrose had already achieved a great deal off his own bat, despite limited financial means. He had set up a Catholic school two miles from Grace Dieu and in 1837 no fewer than three local chapels were consecrated with great ceremony. The first was in the village of Whitwick, the second at Mount Saint Bernard where Ambrose had founded a Cistercian monastery, and the third at Grace Dieu itself.

Like the house, the chapel at Grace Dieu was built by Railton in Tudor Gothic style. Among its embellishments was the first rood screen, separating the choir from the nave, to be erected in England since the sixteenth century. When Pugin first saw it, he embraced Ambrose saying: 'Now at last, I have found a Christian after my own heart.' The two co-operated in 1839 on the building of a new monastery for Mount Saint Bernard close to Grace Dieu and paid for by Shrewsbury.

In the late 1840s Pugin turned his attention to Grace Dieu itself, adding an extra wing and extending the chapel to provide a shrine to the Blessed Sacrament with an elaborate stone canopy. In addition, the interior decorations of the house were given a face-lift.

Pugin also designed the vestments worn by the clergy at Grace Dieu but their striking Gothic style caused an almighty row between those 'Ultramontane' Catholics whose principal concern was respect for papal authority and the 'medievalists' like Pugin and Ambrose. The Ultramontanes saw Pugin's long, wide single-colour chasubles, harking back to an earlier age and in marked contrast to the designs favoured by Rome, as an affront to papal authority. They persuaded the ecclesiastical authorities to reject them. Pugin's misery at this rebuff helped drive him into mental illness and precipitated his death in 1852.

Ambrose's energy and enthusiasm got him into hot water on more than one occasion with the new Catholic hierarchy of bishops, restored by the Pope in England and Wales in 1850 after the post-Reformation turmoil.

The clergy in particular often objected to what they saw as Ambrose's meddling in their affairs while many of the old Catholic families viewed his messianic zeal with distaste, scepticism and even fear. They had survived the previous three centuries of persecution by keeping their heads down and they – correctly – surmised that their tolerant but nevertheless deeply anti-Catholic neighbours were not about to convert in droves.

When Ambrose and his fellow convert George Spencer launched a crusade of prayer for the conversion of England, the ecclesiastical authorities denounced the scheme from the pulpit and labelled Ambrose a dangerous fanatic.

Nevertheless Grace Dieu proved an inspiration to many. William Monsell, the Paymaster General, converted after a visit there. Later created Lord Emly, he joined the tiny band of Catholic peers in the House of Lords.

Ambrose managed the rare feat of befriending both Gladstone and Disraeli, the opposing faces of mid-Victorian England. Gladstone admired Ambrose's religious fervour while Disraeli immortalized him as Eustace Lyle in his novel *Coningsby*.

Though Ambrose was wrong in anticipating a mass return around the country to England's pre-Reformation status as 'Mary's Dowry', he did prove ahead of his time in other matters. In 1857, for example, he helped found the Association for Promoting the Unity of Christendom, a precursor of the modern ecumenical movement. And while his romantic vision of English medieval Catholicism failed to take root in his own church, it did plant the seed of a Catholic style of worship within Anglican ranks which endures to this day.

The death of Ambrose's father in 1862 did not bring any relief from the tremendous financial strain he had placed himself under in his many and varied activities. It allowed him to Gothicize his name – as was fashionable at the time – by the addition of de Lisle. What money he did inherit he spent on renovating in his favoured style the family seat, Garendon Hall. Ambrose had always hated its Palladian austerity, deeming it pagan. He planned to turn it into a moated castle but Pugin's death thwarted this dream.

In the end he turned to Pugin's son Edward to add a pitched roof and a Gothic interior. The mortgage on this alone was so huge that repayments had to be spread over one hundred years. The owner of Garendon paid off the final instalment after the entire house had been pulled down in the 1960s.

When Ambrose inherited Garendon, he passed Grace Dieu to his son, Ambrose-Charles, and his daughter-in-law, Fanny. She reputedly still haunts the house after dying there in a freak accident. A candle set her dress alight and burnt her alive. A memorial window was erected in 1872 in the chapel.

Fanny's husband was the last de Lisle to live at Grace Dieu. After his death in 1883, the house was rented out. In 1933, the Rosminian order took it over as a prep school.

It was an appropriate outcome for a building that was once the centre of the Rosminian mission in Leicestershire. Two de Lisle children currently attend the school but Ambrose would be grieved to hear that Gregorian chant is no longer heard in the chapel, while the Railton rood screen was burnt by an over-enthusiastic priest in the wake of the reforming Second Vatican Council of the 1960s.

Perhaps the best tribute to Ambrose de Lisle came from his fellow Victorian convert, Cardinal John Henry Newman. Though the two quarrelled bitterly in Ambrose's lifetime, Newman reassured his widow: 'No-one can forget him or his great virtues, or his claims on the gratitude of English Catholics...He has in our history a place altogether special.'

MOUNT STUART

ISLE OF BUTE

I look upon our nobility joining the Church of Rome as the greatest
calamity that has ever happened to England. Irrespective of all religious considerations, on which I will not presume to touch, it is an
abnegation of patriotism.

Lady Corisande in 'Lothair' by Disraeli

THE conversion to Catholicism in 1868 of John Patrick Crichton-
Stuart, the third Marquess of Bute, sent such shock-waves through
the country as to make contemporary headlines about royal duchesses and
cabinet ministers abandoning Anglicanism for Rome seem like mere
ripples. There were apocalyptic warnings that Bute – just 21, inheritor of
one of the world's great fortunes and a descendant of the royal house of
Scotland – might start a new trend that would strip the Establishment of its
finest young men.

The dire predictions, of course, proved groundless while the palatial pink
Gothic house of Mount Stuart on the young Marquess's native Isle of Bute
is but one of the many enduring achievements that came in the wake of his

conversion. Bute was indeed one of Britain's greatest ever private patrons of architecture.

Born on the predominantly Presbyterian Scottish island in 1849, Bute inherited his father's thirteen titles and millions while still an infant. By the age of nineteen, an undergraduate at an Oxford which at the time remained effectively out-of-bounds to Catholics, he knew in his heart that he wanted to join the Church of Rome, but bowed to his guardians' wishes that he waited until he was 21. In the interim he busied himself with the restoration and rebuilding of one of his properties, Cardiff Castle, in Gothic fantasy style. Part of the Bute fortune came from the rapid development of Cardiff as a seaport in the nineteenth century.

Three months after coming of age, on the Feast of the Immaculate Conception, Bute was received into the Catholic Church. There were rumours that he had come under Jesuit influence at Oxford, but Bute himself insisted that he had met no priests while at university and had only enlisted Monsignor Capel who received him once the decision was made.

Bute's reasons for converting were straightforward and sincere, as he explained in a later memorandum. He had come, he wrote, 'to see very clearly indeed that the Reformation was in England and Scotland the work neither of God nor of the people, its real authors being, in the former country, a lustful and tyrannical King, and in the latter a pack of greedy, time-serving and unpatriotic nobles. I am also convinced myself...that were I personally to continue...to remain outside the Catholic and Roman Church, I should be making myself an accomplice after the fact in a great national crime.'

A few days after his conversion, he slipped away on pilgrimage to the Holy Land, leaving behind a row that exposed the extent to which Catholics were still regarded as interlopers by much of Britain. One Glasgow evening newspaper pointed to the 'Jesuitism' with which 'his perverted lordship' had denied his conversion the year before and the 'fatal facility' with which he had now been received. The *Glasgow Herald* went one better. 'If, as is most likely,' it thundered, 'this perversion is the result of priestly influences acting upon a weak, ductile and naturally superstitious mind, we may expect a continual eclipse of all intellectual vigour.'

Benjamin Disraeli, born Jewish but turned Anglican, watched with wry amusement the lather produced by Bute's conversion. In 1870 he published a most unflattering portrait both of the Marquess and of the old Catholic families of England in his novel *Lothair*.

On Bute itself, there was outrage at the actions of their Laird. 'They got pictures of me and made them into cockshys,' Bute wrote to a friend, 'and I have had at least one threatening letter from there. Besides that there are no Catholics that I know of and I cannot have a daily Mass.'

In spite of this inhospitable environment, it was Mount Stuart that remained Bute's home in preference to his three other Scottish houses, two in Wales and two in London. It was to Mount Stuart in 1872 that he brought his wife, Gwendoline Fitzalan Howard. She was from that old Catholic world where Bute, unlike his contemporary and fellow convert Ambrose de Lisle, felt most at home.

Their daughter was born there on Christmas Eve 1875, the first of Bute's four offspring. One of their early visitors, Prince Leopold, presents an eccentric though happy portrait of his host, marvelling at the beavers Bute had introduced there. Kangaroos followed later.

Bute was a private man who avoided high society and preferred the company of a small number of – largely Catholic – friends. Often sporting a cloak that looked like a monk's habit and with a full beard, Bute would work away on his translation of the Roman Breviary, or investigate the lives of little-known Scottish saints, or finance the excavating of Lady Chapels around the country. He travelled often to Rome and attended the First Vatican Council in 1870. He was a member of the Zouaves, an international band of Catholics charged with defending the Pope alongside the Swiss Guards.

The eighteenth-century house that Prince Leopold stayed in and where he attended vespers in Bute's private chapel, was destroyed by fire in December 1877. Bute, whose hands one architect claimed 'were never out of the mortar tub', decided to rebuild. In 1879, under the direction of the Edinburgh-based architect Rowand Anderson, Mount Stuart was reborn, an extraordinary cocktail of Venetian, Spanish and French Gothic styles.

The house had not been not completed before Bute's death in 1900, but this delay may explain the Marquess's continuing interest in it. He once remarked that he lost interest in projects once they were finished.

Bute himself played a large part in Mount Stuart's dramatic interior, with a sixty-foot hall inlaid with rare marbles, a sitting room with an astrological ceiling and a vast white marble chapel, described by Lady Lucinda Lambton with her customary vividness as 'permanently aglow with the blood red of its clerestory glass'. The chapel's tower, seen at the northernmost end of the house as you approach it up the long rhododendron drive, is a copy of that at Saragossa Cathedral in northern Spain.

Mount Stuart remains the private home of the present Marquess of Bute.

TICHBORNE HOUSE

I sought my death and found it in my womb,
  I looked for life and saw it was a shade,
I trod the earth and knew it was my tomb,
  And now I die, and now I was but made;
My glass is full, and now my glass is run,
  And now I live, and now my life is done.
From Chideock Tichborne's 'Elegy'
written in the Tower awaiting execution in 1586

WHILE other venerable Catholic families felt specially honoured by royal attention in the nineteenth century following the passage of the Emancipation Act, the Tichbornes found it a dubious privilege. The Prince and Princess of Wales joined the crowds in the High Court in 1871 for one of the most celebrated legal cases of the century, launched by an uneducated butcher from Wagga Wagga in Australia who claimed to be the rightful heir to the Tichborne fortune.

The Grand Duchess Anastasia of his age had in his sights a family name that stretched back to before the Norman Conquest plus the Tichborne estate near Alresford in Hampshire with its graceful Queen Anne-style house complete with Elizabethan wing and recusant chapel. To get his hands on this prize, the butcher claimed to be the long-lost Sir Roger Tichborne.

Young Roger, the apple of his mother's eye, had been educated in France up to his sixteenth birthday in 1845 when he was sent, against her wishes, to Stonyhurst. His subsequent military career was scarcely glittering while his amorous pursuit of his cousin, Kate Doughty, was carried out against her parents' wishes. When they finally agreed to the betrothal it was on condition that Roger went away for three years as a test of his mettle.

He set sail in 1853 for South America and in April of the following year boarded the *Bella* in Rio de Janeiro, bound for New York. The ship was never heard of again. Assuming Roger lost at sea, the Tichborne title passed to his younger brother Alfred on the death of their father, and on Alfred's premature demise in 1866 at the age of 26 to his infant son, Henry.

Roger's mother, the Dowager Lady Tichborne, could never reconcile herself to his loss and began advertising in newspapers around the world in the hope that he had been shipwrecked on some far-flung shore. In 1867 she received a letter from Australia. A family friend who lived there checked out the author and declared him to bear more than a passing resemblance to Roger. And so the butcher from Wagga Wagga and his Irish-born wife travelled to London at Lady Tichborne's expense.

The fact that the Claimant – as he became known – was quite unlike Roger physically, said he had been educated at 'the High School, Southampton' and knew not a word of French, Roger's first language, did not trouble Lady Tichborne. She announced him to be her son, back from the dead, home to take up his inheritance.

He met with sterner opposition from the widowed mother of the infant Sir Henry and her Arundell relatives but nevertheless managed to muster a good deal of support. His – still unexplained – familiarity with the elegant rooms of Tichborne House strengthened his claim while he scored a hit with the tenants on the estate as a man of the people without airs and graces. Such was the publicity this extraordinary case generated that he soon established himself as a national figure.

Part of the Claimant's appeal was his demeanour and evident good nature, but significant too at a time when Catholics, despite changes in the law, were still viewed with suspicion in many parts of the country was the opportunity his quest provided to air long-standing theories of an ancient conspiracy against the nation by recusant Catholics like the Tichbornes and their Arundell cousins.

The death of Lady Tichborne in 1868 was a crushing blow but the Claimant persisted and in May 1871 the case reached court. Representing the Tichbornes was John Duke Coleridge, a future Lord Chief Justice. The fact that his brother had recently converted and become a Jesuit priest only served to fuel rumours of a Catholic plot.

The trial lasted 103 days and the Prince and Princess came to hear the Claimant cross-examined. What finally sunk him was his assertion that he had seduced his beloved Kate before departing for South America. Public opinion may have seen a papal fifth column round every corner but was not prepared to believe that a well-respected and by now happily married county lady would have committed such an unspeakable crime. The court sided with the Tichbornes' barrister and his view that the Claimant was in fact Arthur Orton of East End working-class stock.

With the collapse of his case, the Claimant found himself in the dock, charged with perjury and forgery. He had issued bonds to cover his legal fees, redeemable after his hoped-for victory and signed Sir Roger Tichborne. In February 1874, after a second trial lasting 188 days, the longest ever recorded at that time, he was jailed for 14 years. The sentence produced a public outcry and, though Orton was disbarred from standing for Parliament, he was elected as a People's Candidate in a subsequent by-election.

The Tichbornes took a long time to live down the notoriety. At a celebratory party after the second verdict at nearby Wardour, a footman and a gardener were killed in a freak accident. It was widely held to be divine judgement.

And when in 1913, Sir Henry's son Joseph was getting married, the Claimant's daughter threatened to disrupt the wedding. She landed up in Holloway Prison as a result, but undeterred on her release set up a flower stall outside his London flat and hounded both him and his son Sir Anthony. In the late 1980s, a young Australian branded 'Darren the Baron' by the press turned up at Tichborne to revive Orton's claim. When the police were called, he beat a hasty retreat.

In Victorian times a more positive gloss on the Tichborne name came when Benjamin Disraeli, the future Prime Minister, published his *Curiosities of Literature*. In this 1859 collection he celebrated the work of Chideock Tichborne, executed in 1586 for his part in the Babington Plot which aimed to replace Elizabeth by Mary Queen of Scots. An incurable romantic with little grip on the realities of politics, Chideock appealed to Disraeli as a poetic lover whose last letters to his wife, as well as his celebrated *Elegy* on dying for your faith, are quoted in full in the book.

Chideock was but one of a long line of Tichbornes who refused to break their ties with Rome. In the family vault of the nearby – now Anglican – Church of Saint Andrew are many others who suffered for their failure to conform. A long-standing legend has it that Tichborne House is connected by a secret tunnel to the church, but this has never been uncovered. Indeed the family habitually worshipped in their own chapel, now extensively remodelled but attached to the original Elizabethan wing at the rear of Tichborne.

During renovations after the Second World War various bones and skulls were unearthed under the altar and they were thought to belong to past Tichborne martyrs. The house is also reputedly haunted. Guests who sleep underneath two attic rooms where missionary priests are believed to have sheltered in Elizabethan times report hearing furniture move up there at the dead of night.

When Sir Anthony Tichborne died in 1968 he left no male heirs to his title but bequeathed the house and estate to his eldest daughter Anne Loudon. She continues to live in the old wing and has maintained an annual tradition begun by one of her ancestors back in the twelfth century.

Dame Mabella Tichborne, a renowned benefactor of the poor, begged her husband, Sir Roger, from her deathbed to continue her good works. He, somewhat ungraciously, said that he would only hand out to the poor the product of any fields she could walk round there and then. So the game old lady dragged herself – literally – across 23 acres to make her point.

The field she circled is known as The Crawls and on Lady Day, March 25, the mistress of the house still hands out to local people from the porch steps what is known at the Tichborne Dole. One of the treasures of the house is a seventeenth century painting of this colourful rural scene, set against a backdrop of the original Elizabethan mansion which burnt down in the 1790s. The fire was the direct result, it was said at the time, of the then occupant, Sir Henry Tichborne, discontinuing the Dole and hence incurring Dame Mabella's wrath from beyond the grave.

VISITOR INFORMATION

Warblington is not open to the public.

Hendred is not open to the public.

To visit Stonor: Turn off the M40 motorway at junction 6 and follow the signs for Watlington (B4009). At Watlington head southeast in the direction of Henley-on-Thames, taking the B480 through Stonor. It is open to the public from spring to autumn.

To visit Oxburgh: Head for Stoke Ferry on the A134 between Stradsett and Mundford. At Stoke Ferry follow the signs to Swaffham and in the village of Oxborough you will see signs to Oxburgh Hall. The house is open to the public between March and October.

To visit Broughton: The house is occasionally opened to the public, notably on Bank Holidays, and stands three miles west of Skipton on the A59.

Norbury is a family home and only open to the public by special arrangement with the National Trust.

To visit Baddesley Clinton: Leave the M40 motorway at junction 16 and head north on the A3400 to Hockley Heath. Follow the B4439 east of the town for three miles. The house now belongs to the National Trust and is open to the public.

To visit Hoghton: Follow the A675 southeast of Preston for approximately six miles and then follow the signs to Hoghton. The property is open to the public from Easter Saturday until the end of October. Mondays closed (except for some Bank Holidays); Tuesdays, Wednesdays, Thursdays 11am – 4pm in July and August only; Fridays and Saturdays closed; Sundays 1pm – 5pm.

To visit Mapledurham: Head north from Reading past Caversham on the A4074 and look out for the signposts to Mapledurham. The house is open to the public from Easter Sunday to the last weekend in September.

To visit Coughton: Coughton is located two miles north of Alcester, Warwickshire, on the A435. It is open from April to October.

To visit Wardour Chapel: Take the A30 from Shaftesbury towards Salisbury. At the village of Ludwell, look out for the Castle Inn where you turn left and then follow the signposts for Wardour. The chapel is only open at 10.30am on Sundays for Mass.

To visit Boscobel: Boscobel House is eight miles northwest of Wolverhampton near Brewood, on an unclassified road between the A41 and the A5; Ordnance Survey Landranger (1:50,000) map 127, ref SJ 837083. Open 1 April – 30 September 10am – 6pm, 1 October – 31 March Wednesday – Sunday 10am – 4pm. These dates may change from year to year.

To visit Wardley: The Hall is the private residence of the Bishop of Salford and so is not open to the public. However, visits by groups or associations can be arranged by writing to the Bishop's Secretary at Wardley Hall, Worsley, Manchester M28 2ND.

To visit Traquair: The house is located on the B709 near its junction with the A72. It is open between April and September and in the summer months its Catholic chapel is open for mass once a month.

Ince Blundell stands on the A565 halfway between the centre of Liverpool and the seaside resort of Southport. Mass is said in the chapel each day but the house itself is not open to the public.

To visit Ingatestone: Take the A12 from London towards Chelmsford. Turn off at the Ingatestone exit and follow the signs into the village. Before you reach the shopping centre, look out on your right hand side for Station Lane. Half a mile down is the Hall. Ingatestone is open to the public in the summer months.

To visit Stonyhurst: Leave the M6 at Junction 31 and follow the A59 to Whalley. In the centre of the town, turn left onto the B6246 until its junction with the B6243. Turn left and follow the road to Hurst Green. The school entrance is in the centre of the village. The Church of Saint Peter is used by the local community for Mass on a Sunday and the school is open to the public in August.

Grace Dieu is not open to the public.

While other Bute houses like Cardiff Castle have been given by the family to the nation, **Mount Stuart** remains their private home.

Tichborne is not open to the public, but appointments to visit can be made by writing to Anne Loudon at Tichborne House, near Arlesford, Hampshire. The chapel is used for Sunday Mass. For more details contact the parish priest in Alresford.

SELECT BIBLIOGRAPHY

After Worcester Flight, Allan Fea, London 1904

The Architecture of Northern England, John Martin Robinson, Macmillan 1986

The Architecture of Southern England, John Julius Norwich, Macmillan 1985

Baddesley Clinton, The Rev. Henry Norris, London 1897

Brideshead Revisited, Evelyn Waugh, various editions

Cardinal Hume and the Changing Face of English Catholicism, Peter Stanford, Geoffrey Chapman 1993

The Catholic Families, Mark Bence-Jones, Constable 1992

Catholic Lancashire, J. A.Hilton, Phillimore 1994

The Claimant, Michael Gilbert, Constable 1957

Curious Houses , Lady Lucinda Lambton, Chatto & Windus 1988

The Dukes of Norfolk, John Martin Robinson, Oxford 1982

Edmund Campion, Evelyn Waugh, Longmans 1935

The English Catholic Community 1570-1850, John Bossy, Darton, Longman & Todd 1975

Faith and Family: The Life and Circle of Ambrose Phillips de Lisle, Margaret Pawley, Canterbury Press 1993

Forgotten Shrines, Dom Bede Camm, McDonald & Evans 1910

Henry VIII, J. J. Scarisbrick, Eyre & Spottiswoode 1968

History of Peebleshire (Volume Two), J. W. Buchan, Glasgow 1925

The History of Wardley Hall, Henry Vaughan, Hart-Davis 1908

Ince Blundell Hall, Captain and Mrs Weld-Blundell, privately published 1956

John Gerard: Autobiography of an Elizabethan, Longmans 1951

The Life of Robert Southwell, Poet and Martyr, Christopher Devlin, Longmans 1956

The Marquess of Bute, the Right Rev. Sir David Hunter Blair, London 1921

Mary Queen of Scots, Lady Antonia Fraser, Weidenfeld, 1969

Newman and His Age, Sheridan Gilley, Darton, Longman & Todd 1990

Old Catholic Lancashire (two volumes), Dom FO Blundell OSB, Longmans 1925

Oxburgh Hall, Henry Bedingfeld, National Trust 1987

Pugin, Michael Trappes-Lomax, Sheed and Ward 1932

Recusant History – the journal of the Catholic Record Society – held in its entirety in
    the Catholic Central Library, Francis Street, London SW1

The Reformation and the English People, J. J. Scarisbrick, Blackwell 1984

Robert Weir Schultz, Gavin Stamp, Curwen Press 1981

The Royal Miracle, A. M. Broadley, London 1912

St Omer to Stonyhurst, Hubert Chadwick SJ, Burns & Oates 1961

Secret Hiding Places, Michael Hodgetts, Veritas 1989

The Sequel to Catholic Emancipation, B. Ward, London 1915

Stonor, R. J. Stonor, R. H. Johns 1952

Stonyhurst College 1593-1993, T. E. Muir, James & James 1992

The Stripping of the Altars, Eamonn Duffy, Yale 1992

The Tempests of Broughton Hall, M. E. Lancaster, privately published 1987

Thames Valley Papists, Tony Hadland, privately published 1992

The Tichborne Claimant, Douglas Woodruff, Hollis and Carter 1957

Tudor England, S. T. Bindoff, various editions.

Vaux of Harrowden, Godfrey Anstruther, R. H. Johns 1953

Wardour: A Short History, Philip Caraman SJ, privately published 1984

INDEX

(Many Catholic families used the same Christian name for eldest sons in successive genera-
tions. For each family listed, individual Christian names have only been given once unless
there is a variation in title. Hence if you are looking for, say, a Robert Tempest, follow all the
references until you find the Robert Tempest who coincides with the period you are studying.)